"Masterfully weaving less  past, Steve Gray and J. D church for returning to C reminds us that Christ's ever-present power can viduals, regions, and even nations when we humbly exchange our sins and traditions for His holy ways."

Josh Adkins, cofounder of Sent Ones, author of *Heaven Here*

"Join two seasoned authors who have witnessed the power of revival firsthand as they challenge you to break free from the status quo and pursue the extraordinary life God has in store for you. Get ready to be inspired, convicted, and stirred. There is more!"

Dr. Michael L. Brown, host of *The Line of Fire* broadcast and author of *Revival or We Die*

"In this book, Steve Gray and J. D. King—pioneers of the Smithton Outpouring—deliver a life-changing message. With Spirit-led insight, they stir up our thirst for God and remind us of His transformative power. This book isn't just an inspiring read; it's an encounter that will profoundly impact you."

Randy Clark, president of Global Awakening

"Steve Gray and J. D. King share firsthand accounts of the Smithton Outpouring, an extraordinary move of God, illustrating their experiences with the narrative of Gideon, a man used by God to bring renewal to the nation of Israel. Just as God transformed a vulnerable man hiding in fear into a warrior, Gray and King provide valuable insights along with prophetic revelations that will embolden readers to pursue their own destiny of revival and spiritual empowerment."

Connie Dawson, PhD, professor of church and revival history, Global Awakening Theological Seminary

"*Mighty like Gideon* draws on a familiar story from the Old Testament, reworking the lessons into a modern-day road map for spiritual growth. Gray and King have proven track records, writing as men who have spent time in the presence of God. Their book contains revelatory insights that will enrich the life of any believer."

William L. DeArteaga, author of *Quenching the Spirit* and *Forgotten Power*

"*Mighty like Gideon* is a brilliant collaboration of two ministers who have seen historic revival and awakening in their church and have experienced fresh outpouring in their own lives. These two men of God share personal, vulnerable insights of God's power in their lives and their responses. A powerful journey!"

Dr. Mike Hutchings, Global Awakening associate, president of God Heals PTSD Foundation

"Steve Gray and J. D. King have crafted a masterpiece. Their combined wisdom, from a lifetime of battles and personal experiences, is a priceless gift. *Mighty like Gideon* is a refreshing and inspiring read. I highly recommend it for anyone ready to embark on a journey of personal growth and transformation."

Daniel Kolenda, evangelist, president of Christ for all Nations, lead pastor of Nations Church

"Gray and King skillfully call us to recognize that what we need today is not spiritual superstars or special revelations but, rather, a contrite heart and a desire to hear God's Word."

Robert Menzies, director of the Asian Center for Pentecostal Theology

"The biblical story of Gideon and the God encounter that transformed his life have always been inspirational. J. D. King and Steve Gray unpack and amplify Gideon's adventures in a way that will challenge every believer to crave the presence and power of God. A great read by two great men."

Larry Martin, DMin, missionary evangelist, author, historian

"This is a call for people to take their rightful place in the kingdom of God. We must walk in alignment with God's purposes. There is a crossroads, a defining moment that must take place at waters meant not only for refreshing but also consecration. Steve Gray and J. D. King release a wealth of knowledge for all who thirst for rivers of living water and long to prepare for, partner with, and steward a great move of God in our day."

Jennifer A. Miskov, PhD, revival historian, founding director of
School of Revival and Writing in the Glory

"Steve and J. D. have written a masterpiece from the life of Gideon that surpassed my greatest expectations. What I loved most wasn't their great knowledge but their heartfelt honesty and humility! If you desire a greater encounter and connection with the Lord, this book is for you."

Brent Rudoski, pastor of Faith Alive Family Church, author of
Mercy Triumphs Over Judgment and *Think on This*

"I am so grateful to God for Steve Gray and J. D. King's book *Mighty like Gideon*. Even more than the book are the men who wrote it. These men walked in and through the very things they write about and have come out on the other side to give language, clarity, and courage to a new generation so that we can enter into everything God has for us. This book is a gift for this generation."

Corey Russell, author and speaker, CoreyRussell.org

"Revival historian J. D. King and revival pastor Steve Gray have tasted the fires of landscape-changing Holy Spirit outpouring. They are revival practitioners, so when they write about the subject, I pay careful attention. This incredible book gives you powerful and practical Bible secrets to ensure that revival does not remain a one-time memory but is cultivated as your everyday lifestyle!"

Larry Sparks, publisher for Destiny Image

MIGHTY
LIKE
GIDEON

MIGHTY LIKE GIDEON

REVIVED AND BATTLE-READY AT YOUR RIVER OF TESTING

STEVE GRAY
AND J. D. KING

Chosen

a division of Baker Publishing Group
Minneapolis, Minnesota

Published by Chosen Books
Minneapolis, Minnesota
ChosenBooks.com

Chosen Books is a division of
Baker Publishing Group, Grand Rapids, Michigan

Printed in the United States of America

Library of Congress Cataloging-in-Publication Data

Names: Gray, Steve, author. | King, J. D. (Jerry Don), author.

Title: Mighty like Gideon : revived and battle-ready at your river of testing / Steve Gray and J.D. King.

Description: Minneapolis, Minnesota : Chosen Books, a division of Baker Publishing Group, [2025] | Includes bibliographical references.

Identifiers: LCCN 2024023255 | ISBN 9780800772987 (paper) | ISBN 9780800773076 (casebound) | ISBN 9781493448852 (ebook)

Subjects: LCSH: Gideon (Biblical judge) | Bible. Judges. | Revivals—United States. | Christianity—United States.

Classification: LCC BS580.G5 G73 2025 | DDC 222/.32—dc23/eng/20240814

LC record available at https://lccn.loc.gov/2024023255

Cover design by InsideOut Creative Arts, Inc.

Baker Publishing Group publications use paper produced from sustainable forestry practices and postconsumer waste whenever possible.

25 26 27 28 29 30 31   7 6 5 4 3 2 1

Bobbie, your love and support have been my strength. This book exists because of you.

—J. D. King

To my wife, Kathy—your unwavering support and guidance have shaped the words within these pages. This book stands as a tribute to our shared journey and to your influence on my life and work. Thank you for your wisdom, strength, and input, which have made this book possible.

—Steve Gray

CONTENTS

INTRODUCTION

The River Beckons

Where the river flows everything will live.

Ezekiel 47:9 NIV

Picture yourself on a river's edge, near the rollicking waters. Every ripple gracefully bends and swirls, pulsating with life. If you are feeling parched, the bubbling streams beckon, inviting you to satisfy your thirst. The cleansing flow never fails to bring relief to those who are cracked and dry.

The river dances with a rhythm, breathing new life into every creature that drinks from its waters. Its flowing streams become a guide, transporting weary travelers into uncharted realms of beauty and wonder.

It's no wonder that people often turn to the metaphor of rivers to describe a marvelous move of God. The outpourings of the Holy Spirit, like these bubbling streams, captivate all who witness them.

For over a quarter of a century, Steve Gray and I have drunk from these living streams. While the two of us have completely different backgrounds and experiences, our lives have been inter-twined through the glorious work of the Holy Spirit.

God sparked a fire in Gray in 1996, and he became a catalyst for a revival movement that broke open in rural Missouri. It became known as the "Smithton Outpouring." I ventured into these meetings not long after they began, seeking a fresh touch from God—as well as a mentor. Gray and I have now worked side by side for over twenty-five years.

The lessons and spiritual strategies that we have learned are being brought together in this book. Drawing inspiration from Gideon's story in Judges 6–8, the two of us wanted to discuss the Lord's ability to purify, rejuvenate, and transport believers into uncharted realms of spiritual growth. We are excited to share some of the lessons we have learned while standing in the Lord's presence.

The pages of this book are filled with history, Scripture, and firsthand testimonies. The assortment of chapters that we wrote reflects the outlook of two generations—and voices—unified in the pursuit of a lasting spiritual legacy. We set out to offer keys to help you unlock your own spiritual destiny.

This is a pivotal hour, and we believe that every Christian is being summoned to drink from the living waters. In the face of adversity, fear, and suffering, the river of God is beckoning you. So, this book is an invitation to come to the river and plunge into the life-giving streams of the Lord. In this defining moment, embrace the opportunity to be refreshed, revitalized, and transformed.

—J. D. King

PART 1

PREPARING

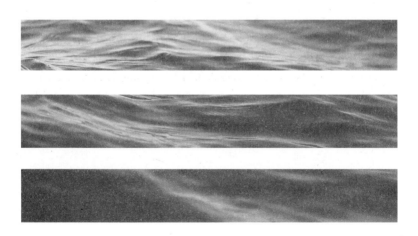

1

SUMMONED TO THE RIVER

Do You Want Something More?

J. D. KING

In the spring of 1996, the flood tides of revival burst forth in the quaint town of Smithton, Missouri. With a population of only 532, the community wasn't even on most maps. People don't expect a movement of God to begin in a place like that, but the Lord has a way of disrupting our assumptions.

At the heart of this small community stood Steve Gray. After years of dedicated service as a pastor, he was spiritually parched. He was yearning for a breakthrough, but it hadn't come. Despite the temptation to resign, his deep love for the congregation kept him from walking away.

News of a fiery revival in Pensacola, Florida, had reached Gray's ears, and he made the decision to travel there. At the time, crowds were coming to Pensacola from all over to receive a fresh touch from the Lord. Many yearned for revival, but Gray was only looking for survival.

After spending ten days in the Florida panhandle, praying and listening to God, Gray made his way back to Missouri. He didn't feel as though anything had changed, but the Lord was working. Gray was on the edge of something marvelous.

When Gray entered the sanctuary of his congregation at 6:12 p.m. on March 24, 1996, surges of power rushed through his body like electricity. He raised his arms and began leaping. One person in attendance said, "I watched Pastor Steve go twirling into the air. A strong wave began rolling over the people from the front to the back."

The heaviness lifted off Gray, and joy returned. A woman remarked that the people responded en masse during worship, filling the space in front of the platform to the aisles all the way to the back of the auditorium. She added that the presence of the Lord was so thick that people were trembling on all sides, and that everyone from six to sixty—teens and middle-aged—all collapsed and wept under the power of God.

The atmosphere of the building was tangibly thick with the presence of the Lord. Some were experiencing immense joy, and others began weeping. Families began to huddle together and cry out to the Lord. What was sparked on the evening of March 24 ushered Steve Gray and his congregation into an extraordinary move of God.

Soon the little church, hidden in the cornfields, became a pilgrimage point for tens of thousands of Christians. The stories of what was transpiring were arresting. As people encountered the goodness and glory of the Lord, everything changed. Reports were spreading far and wide about the wondrous move of God. Thousands were being swept up in this marvelous work—including me.

I remember how struck I was when I read a report from an evangelist who had attended one of the services. He wanted to tell everyone what he had seen and heard:

I witnessed people weeping, moaning, wailing, and crying out in repentance. I saw people falling under the power of God, and bodies were piled up everywhere in the room. Most of those who had fallen were never even touched by anyone—God had done it all. The air was so thick with the presence of God that I had to get on my hands and knees just to get some air. Let me tell you, the weight of the Lord's glory was overwhelming.[1]

The crowds swelled in this tiny town in the middle of nowhere. Some of the visitors would begin lining up in the early afternoon to ensure that they had a seat in the crowded sanctuary. Occasionally, the vehicles arriving stretched for two and a half miles—bumper-to-bumper. Thousands were visiting the meetings, but even more were intrigued by the reports. Jesus was clearly changing lives.

National publications like *Charisma*, *Christianity Today*, and *Newsweek*, as well as newspapers such as the *San Francisco Chronicle* and the *Kansas City Star*, documented the extraordinary gatherings—providing a firsthand account of the passion and fervor.[2]

Samuel Autman, a journalist from the *St. Louis Post-Dispatch*, made the pilgrimage to Smithton and shared his gripping report:

> The prayer sessions seem violent. Many worshipers pray, weep, tremble and are knocked to the floor by what they consider to be the hand of God. By evening's end, this room will resemble a battlefield littered with human bodies, many supine on the gray carpet, "slain in the Spirit." They say they are so overcome by the Holy Spirit, they shake, quake, roll, jerk or even faint. Within minutes, a jubilant energy fills the room, almost like electricity. The faithful believe the Spirit has come with power to heal broken hearts, to transform lives and get them on the road to glory.[3]

I remember another occasion when a television reporter was also in attendance—with notebook and pen in hand. As the worship intensified, he couldn't maintain his composure. He dropped all his belongings on the floor and wept. He had come to observe the story, but suddenly became part of it.

The Kingdom of God operates in such a fascinating way. It invites you to witness something extraordinary. As you are immersed in the glory, however, something unexpected begins to transpire. First you are merely a spectator, but then you become fully immersed in it. The invitations lead to revelations. The living waters have this amazing way of drawing us in, making us not only onlookers but active participants.

During this time, I was a Bible college student trying to understand some of what God was doing in the world. The stories coming out of this rural town were hard to dismiss. I joined crowds from the Midwest, large coastal cities, and other parts of the globe to seek the Lord in a place in the middle of nowhere.

All who came were squeezed into rickety folding chairs—shoulder to shoulder. Cracked and dry people, like me, were being continually refreshed. We raised our hands and sang with such intensity that our voices could be heard for miles. What was happening in that small town could not be overlooked. In an out-of-the-way place, the thirsty were being refreshed and restored.

By the river's edge, God was teaching us profound lessons—stirring a sense of something greater. With every sip from the wellspring, our thirst for Jesus grew even deeper. All around me, dry and thirsty souls were being made new. When you come near the river, life finds a new rhythm.

The Need-of-Nothing Attitude

I can still picture that moment when a passenger van rolled into the Smithton parking lot. It carried some seminary students who had traveled a considerable distance. As these men strolled into the building, an unmistakable air of condescension surrounded them. Their snickers and knowing looks caught my attention. They were poking fun at the zeal of the rural congregants. Although these students were being trained in the nuances of Scripture, they seemed to have little thirst for the living waters. As the service began, the men remained standoffish. As other attendees stood, the seminarians remained seated. Melodies echoed through the room as hundreds passionately worshiped. The atmosphere crackled with energy, but this seemed to have no effect on these young academics. Amid the fervor, each one remained stoic—untouched by the lives being transformed around them.

Becoming a dynamic, Spirit-led believer is about more than acquiring knowledge. Doctrine matters, but doctrine alone will not take you where you need to go. These pious men dismissed the less-educated worshipers in the room. Little did they realize that these seemingly simple people had a deeper grasp of Jesus than they did.

Christians were not designed to be mere spectators; we are participants. The sons and daughters of the Most High are supposed to reflect His divine image here on earth. In the New Testament, the apostle Paul reiterates that Christ followers "can see and reflect the glory of the Lord. And the Lord—who is the Spirit—makes us more and more like him as we are changed into his glorious image" (2 Corinthians 3:18 NLT).

To genuinely embody the Jesus image, we must invest not only our minds, but also our bodies and emotions. The entirety of who we are needs to be brought into this concern. Mere agreement in thought won't be enough. We're being summoned to be fully immersed in the realities of the unfolding Kingdom.

That night in Smithton, as the service reached its conclusion, I had the opportunity to talk with Jim, one of the seminarians who had joined us. Though friendly, he was a little shaky when he talked to me. I could tell that he wasn't entirely comfortable. Jim said, "My classmates and I felt compelled to drive out here and witness this phenomenon firsthand. I've never experienced a service quite like this. Someone referred to this as 'the river.' So, I guess we wanted to come out and watch people drink."

Jim and his colleagues had journeyed to the countryside to observe and evaluate those along the river. What they witnessed gave them plenty to talk about. Yet they spent so much time gawking at people that they never considered that they needed the waters too.

Why do so many churchgoers assume that it's someone else who needs a touch from the Lord? Are we blind to our own spiritual stagnation? John the Revelator warned believers in the city of Laodicea about their complacency and pride: "You say, 'I am rich. I have everything I want. I don't need a thing!' And you don't realize that you are wretched and miserable and poor and blind and naked" (Revelation 3:17 NLT).

The lingering "need-of-nothing" attitude in Christian circles is keeping many from experiencing a fuller manifestation of glory. I don't know what it stems from, but it seems that a substantial number of Spirit-filled believers mistakenly believe they've outgrown drinking from the life-giving waters. We certainly need to build our lives on the Word of God and understand who we are in Christ, but we can't embrace the notion that we have already arrived. We all need a fresh touch from time to time.

Some are blind to their own spiritual lack and imagine that they don't need anything from God. They don't seem to understand that everyone needs a drink. I have a charismatic acquaintance who recently said, "J. D., I don't need revival; I am revival! If you truly knew who you are in Christ, you would realize that all that other stuff is a bunch of hype and noise." I understand this person's point, but over time this kind of outlook could lead to a smug satisfaction.

Every believer needs to return to the edge of the river to drink from time to time. I don't care who you are, the vitality of a fresh move of God is something that we never move past. The rivers of revival are not passé; they are a vital part of what the Lord is doing in this hour.

Dry Seasons

Over time, Spirit-filled believers can forget what the invigorating waters taste like. I've spoken with hundreds who have drunk from these streams in the past, but they have since lost their sense of the beauty and wonder. Men and women who were once brimming with living water now find themselves in an endless dry season—and somehow, they aren't bothered by it.

I remember a colleague saying, "We once had rivers of life and thousands of thirsty souls, but now it feels like a dark era. J. D., I've been watching carefully, but there's no sign of refreshing on the horizon." I couldn't believe a Spirit-filled believer would talk like this. Where was this person's hope? Sadly, I've encountered many who share this same outlook.

Conversations with Christians today seem to revolve around politics, societal issues, or financial concerns. Many who were once endued with power are now convinced that the river has run dry and the stagnant fields will never blossom again. These men and women can't envision anything good happening in our time. Every time that I encounter this, it breaks my heart.

I understand the fears believers are grappling with. I've seen many of the same news reports they have. I know unsettling things are taking place in our world. Yet all that we are seeing in the media is only part of the story. It may seem as if things will always remain dry, but they won't. Droughts don't last forever. I love what the prophet Samuel proclaimed to some misguided men years ago: "It's the dry season, isn't it? But I will pray, and the LORD will send thunder and rain" (1 Samuel 12:17 GNT). We should adopt a similar mindset. Even in stagnant times, we can trust in the Lord's goodness. Sooner or later, things will turn around by the hand of God.

In times of drought, when adversaries are poised to attack, navigating conflicts may not be the most pleasant endeavor. Yet, amid these trials is an opportunity for advancement. Instead of standing idly by, believers should drink from the refreshing stream.

In moments of crisis, let's drink from the living waters, for they have the power to invigorate every aspect of our lives.

Rivers of Revival

Outpourings of the Holy Spirit are often linked to the imagery of rivers and streams. Frequently, I find myself revisiting the experiences I've had in the waters. Standing alongside my pastor, Steve Gray, I've been privileged to witness remarkable moments—occasions when God brought salvation, healing, and deliverance. In the river, Jesus touches many lives.

In my mind's eye, I remember thousands coming face-to-face with the glory of the Lord. In restaurants, parking lots, and crowded churches, thousands of men and women have been powerfully touched. I also recall the blank expressions of the obstinate—individuals who lingered at the river's edge but never fully immersed themselves in the stream.

The seminary student's comment about simply observing others drinking at the river has lingered in my mind over the years. It reminded me of the story of Gideon and his ragtag army from Judges 6. We can glean many spiritual lessons from this account.

Gideon's story unfolds as ancient Israel faces a pivotal moment. Losing sight of their God-given identity, the people turned in the wrong direction. Scripture describes the dire situation: "the land was stripped bare," and the people were "reduced to starvation" (Judges 6:5–6 NLT). As the people of God lost sight of the Lord, the land grew dry and barren.

As Gideon's recruits approached the stream, ready to battle Israel's oppressors, questions arose. Who among them would dare to taste the waters, and how would they choose to drink? Ultimately, their modus operandi on the banks of the stream would determine who among them would be chosen to fight with Gideon, and who would be sent home. Shorelines serve not only as places for refreshment, but also as sites for consecration and commissioning.

In Israel's darkest hour, God raised up thirsty warriors willing to advance under His guidance. They mastered the art of listening, praying, and drinking. When God begins to move, the ordinary becomes extraordinary.

This account provides so many poignant lessons for those who want to prevail in the deeper things of God. Among other things, one might have to walk through challenging times of preparation. Are you still laying the right kind of foundation? The thirsty will have to learn how to posture themselves. Ultimately, believers will have to discover how to carry what the Spirit is birthing within them. None of this is easy, but the living waters are always worth it. Scripture declares; "Taste and see that the LORD is good" (Psalm 34:8 NLT). How thirsty are you?

River Tales

Over the last several years, Steve Gray and I have been blessed to drink deeply from the living waters. Over this time, people have urged us to write about our experiences and disclose some of the stories and biblical principles we have learned. Recently, this idea came up again, and the two of us committed to writing this book together.

Throughout our journey, the story of Gideon has resonated deeply with both of us. Its richness extends beyond documenting encounters with God; it offers tangible, actionable steps for walking in the things of the Spirit. Steve and I wanted to delve beneath the surface, both in Gideon's story and in ours—plumbing the depths where Scripture, spiritual encounters, and practical actions intersect. We want to tell some of our stories and highlight truths that might bring you into a place of understanding and empowerment. Our desire is that this would be more than a book. We want it to become an invitation—a beckoning call—to drink from the Lord's life-giving streams.

As you flip through these pages, allow the current to carry you away, drawing you into the mighty river itself. Much like Gideon's recruits and the seminarians in Smithton, we will invariably find ourselves at the water's edge. The question remains: Will you drink or remain a spectator? As you stand near the waters, what will your choice be? The future is shaped by your decisions. What are you going to do when you find yourself standing on the river's edge?

2

A TRUE ASSESSMENT

Are Things Moving in the Wrong Direction?

STEVE GRAY

People don't always see things moving in the wrong direction. The American church in the 1980s and '90s got caught up in a marketing mindset. Many preachers started sounding like corporate executives trying to make a sale instead of servants trying to save lives. At this same time, Christian music was a growing industry, tempting many recording artists to create crossover hits that would move them out of religion.

It was a profitable and costly season. It was lucrative financially, but it came with a high price spiritually. Slowly, the symptoms we believers had left behind—like divorce, alcohol, infidelity, and entertainment—crept back in. For me, it was like watching a spider weaving a web to catch unsuspecting prey. The excesses, heartless worship, and televangelist scandals shook some. Still, they were not stirred enough to stand up to the new definition of success defined by numbers and money. People overlooked the selfish pursuits, pride, and the get-in-get-out, fast-food flair church.

I felt the pressure to become like a cast member in Hans Christian Andersen's fable, "The Emperor's New Clothes." The emperor was naked. Who in the Church wants to be the little boy who exposes the delusion by shouting, "The Emperor is not wearing anything at all!"? We lied to ourselves and each other. We pranced in pretend clothes while miserable, blind, and naked.

Today, much is the same. We need truth tellers to assess who and what we have become. God is talking to us, but we stopped listening when He didn't say what we wanted to hear. God's prophetic signs still point to loyalty, sacrifice, and dying to self. The modern Church has so distanced itself from the Word of God, however, that self-love has replaced godliness.

Not Listening

During the time of Gideon, the people of Israel had forgotten the word of the Lord. They turned away from righteousness and became wicked, worshiping false gods. Israel bowed before Baal, the god of the neighboring nations.

As a result of their waywardness, God removed His favor. Israel fell into the hands of the Midianites. Oppressive poverty followed. We can see their condition from the book of Judges: "The Israelites did evil in the LORD's sight. So the LORD handed them over to the Midianites for seven years" (Judges 6:1 NLT).

Selfishness and sin create a culture of destruction. The Lord takes away His blessings when His people get entangled in the world. When Jesus is no longer the focus, we lose the favor we once had. At first, the loss is gradual and barely noticeable. God's love can still strike us through a song or a sermon. Suddenly, however, we wake up from spiritual slumber and wonder what happened. We need a revival that grants grace and favor and saves us from ourselves.

During Gideon's time, Israel lived in poverty, disease, and political oppression. Still blinded, the people didn't see their hand in the nation's collapse. To experience restoration, they would have to assess their part in what they had become and what they must do to live free.

God sent a prophet with a clear message: "I drove out your enemies and gave you their land. I told you, 'I am the LORD your God. You must not worship the gods of the Amorites, in whose land you now live.' But you have not listened to me" (Judges 6:9–10 NLT).

Our crime is similar. The Kingdom of God is here, but we have no time for it. We are satisfied, without the need for change. We comfort ourselves with religious titles to compensate for our lack of zeal. We have wayward Christians, lukewarm Christians, and backslidden Christians. Yet there are no subtitles with God. You won't see the lukewarm, disobedient, or backslidden in heaven. Only faithful servants arrive in glory.

Current church policies are all about comfort and accommodation, while promoting weakness as the norm. Sermons come with a time clock, hurried along by those with something better to do. I want to stand with people with nothing better to do, because they know there is nothing better to do: "Better is one day in your courts than a thousand elsewhere" (Psalm 84:10 NIV).

Why Can't We Be Blessed?

Abraham came before God and asked if Ishmael, his son by the handmaiden Hagar, could be his heir: "Abraham said to God, 'If only Ishmael might live under your blessing!'" (Genesis 17:18 NIV).

God had promised Abraham a son in his old age. What was wrong with Ishmael? Wouldn't he do? He's a son, and there was no way to make him more of a son. The promise to Abraham, however, was not just a son. If that were the case, Ishmael would qualify. The key to the promised son was not just that he would be born, but *how* that son would be born.

Abraham called himself dead at one hundred years old, and Sarah as good as dead. Ishmael was born in the ordinary way, through a young servant girl. The promised son, Isaac, was born out of the dead reproductive bodies of Abraham and Sarah. Why was this so important to God?

God was painting a prophetic picture of the coming Messiah and the Resurrection. Jesus was crucified. Jesus was dead. His lifeless body lay in a tomb made for the dead. By the power of the Holy Spirit, He became alive a second time, with a glorified body that will never die.

In 2008, revival broke out again, and the Kansas City Revival began with four services a week for over three years. Besides the regular services, the Friday night service was broadcast live for ninety minutes in every state and worldwide. As in Smithton, lines were formed early every weekend by those determined to get a place in the packed auditorium.

Those touched by the fire of God returned to their churches, ready for revival. Some in those congregations who had never watched or attended our services were confused by the joy and freedom these new revivalists brought home with them. Their revived church buddies wanted something new, while the rest of the congregation was baffled, as Abraham had been about Ishmael, and asked, "What's wrong with our church?"

The Promised Bride

Abraham loved Ishmael. God loved Ishmael. God loves the people in your church. Hopefully, your church is a good church. "Good," however, often stands in the way of "God." Here is how a good church works: Put together a team. Make people comfortable with themselves. Introduce good friends. Tell them what they want to hear. Follow the pattern of corporate America, and you've got a successful church. Of course it's a good church; it's just not the one promised to Jesus. Ephesians 5:27 reveals that God promises

Jesus a radiant, holy Church without spots, wrinkles, blemishes, or anything else.

Look realistically, with compassion and without criticism, at what has happened with "good" churches. Pastors deal daily with the depressed, angry, fearful, and doubtful. These aren't the unsaved finding their way into the light. No, these are the Bible-believing, church-attending Christians.

Here is the Bible's description of the Church to be presented to Jesus: He will have a Bride and "present *her to himself as a radiant church*, without stain or wrinkle or any other blemish, but holy and blameless" (Ephesians 5:27 NIV, emphasis added). This is the Church promised to Jesus.

In "good" churches, believers are so broken that sermons are now group therapy. Church people come to stretch out on the Jesus couch and learn why they aren't happy. Are there exceptions? Of course there are, but if a church service runs like a repair shop for broken-down jalopies needing a jump start every week, then that church is not the exception.

Fortune 500 businesses, political think tanks, or the self-absorbed world of social media can't give birth to what God has destined. We don't need more voices teaching us, "Just give the people what they want, and they will come." It's not about what the masses want. It's not about making new friends or how people feel about life, love, or themselves. It is all about what God wants.

I remember standing up one Sunday morning with this greeting: "Welcome to Revive Church, a wonderful place where your opinion doesn't matter." Of course, this was an exaggeration that got a few laughs, but it does make a point. Our opinions have turned the Church into an unpresentable hag, with many lovers of Jesus needing constant attention and affirmation that they are special and loved.

Paul used the term *Bride* for the Church for a reason. With the help of other women, a Hebrew bride would often spend a year preparing for the wedding. She would learn beauty secrets for her skin and hair. Most of all, she would develop the inner beauty only a wife can bring to a relationship. During her time of preparation, a young woman's loyalty and thoughts were for only one man. She became more beautiful and more radiant as the time for her presentation to her husband drew near. She was holy, set apart for one man only, a picture of the Bride promised to Jesus.

Want to be a bride? Let's not forget that we are part of the Church Triumphant, where losers become winners and victims become victorious. Yet many in the Church forget just that. I'm not talking about bad people. I'm talking about busy people who want it all and refuse the call to live separate from the world. They are like circus folks trying to spin as many plates on a stick as possible. The Hebrew bride was busy preparing for married life. Only one plate was spinning in her heart, the one for her husband.

Words like being *separate* and *holy* are not heard that much today. We sing many songs about holiness, wondering what it is. Being set apart for God's use only is holiness. Preaching with a bridelike attitude is offensive to some churches. The term *Bride of Christ* is often thrown around in some circles by those who lack understanding. Attending a wedding doesn't make you a bride. Attending a church doesn't make you *the* Bride.

A True Assessment

Nehemiah, a devout Jewish official in the Persian court, desired to see Jerusalem rebuilt. The city was in ruins. He first needed to assess the damage before the work could begin. Nehemiah said that in the middle of the night, he "went out through the Valley Gate toward the Jackal Well and the Dung Gate, examining the walls of Jerusalem, which had been broken down, and its gates, which had been destroyed by fire" (Nehemiah 2:13 NIV). Nehemiah did more than evaluate the damage to Israel. He also assessed his heart, damaged by the Jerusalem crowd that overlooked the devastated city. God placed it on his heart to restore the glory of Israel by rebuilding the Temple.

Centuries later, the disciples walked with Jesus through the Temple area. They marveled at the magnificent buildings. Magnificent buildings, like big churches, can deceive, giving a sense of security that all is well. Jesus' message was the opposite: All was not well (see Matthew 24:1–2). The ruling religious were hypocrites. Rome would come as a tool of righteous judgment. The impressive walls and gates would be utterly destroyed by fire.

In the New Testament, people are the temple of the Holy Spirit. Sadly, multitudes live in spiritual ruin, with broken-down gates and burned walls. Ministers in the trenches know all too well the struggles, heartache, and regrets that plague the people of the pews.

The children of the light are hurting, worn, discouraged travelers searching for answers. They need refreshing and renewal, and they need revival. These "people temples," not built with hands, should be holy, acceptable, vibrant, full of faith, and full of the life of Jesus.

Haggai's Assessment

The prophet Haggai correctly assessed the problem in his day and brought the answer:

> Now this is what the LORD Almighty says: "Give careful thought to your ways. You have planted much, but harvested little. You eat, but never have enough. You drink, but never have your fill. You put on clothes, but are not warm. You earn wages, only to put them in a purse with holes in it."
>
> Haggai 1:5–6 NIV

Haggai asked the people to consider their ways. Their lives didn't make sense. They planted much, but got little. That shouldn't happen. They had jobs and earned wages, but where did the money go? The devil didn't do it. Their enemies didn't cause it. God did it. God made life go wrong so they could make it right.

The Babylonians had destroyed Solomon's Temple. The rebuilding had started, and then it stopped for sixteen years. A group of nobodies who talked like somebodies had said it wasn't time to build God's house. The people found time to build their own houses, however, which was the source of all their trouble. The Lord blew away their money and called for a drought. Haggai, sent from God, brought the fix: Take care of God's house, and God will take care of you. Your money will return, heaven's gates will open wide, and trouble will end.

Today, we live with the same symptoms. While sermons promise blessings and joy, people live in lack, fear, stress, and helpless disappointment. This can all be fixed. Give the Kingdom of God first place now. Our temples of the Holy Spirit need repair, but repair is possible. The Church needs preparation lessons and an understanding of the Bible's picture of Jesus coming for His Bride.

3

FERVENT CRIES

Desperate Prayer Sets the Stage
for Breakthrough

J. D. KING

In moments of desperation, the hurt and needy lean into prayer. When facing ugliness and pain, people often turn their voice toward heaven. In the dark night of the soul, intercession arises.

For the longest time, I struggled with prayer. Interceding alongside others wasn't so difficult, but the moment I tried to have a heart-to-heart with God, things usually took a nose dive. When I opened my mouth, I would get entangled in anxiety and self-analysis. I knew there were deeper places to go in the Spirit, but I struggled getting there.

Like ancient Israel, I was often my own worst enemy. I overlooked crucial matters until they escalated into crises. Hoping for a quick turnaround, I would utter a few words and hope that the Lord would clean up my messes. I knew prayer wasn't supposed to work like this, but I did it anyway.

Having sown seeds of destruction, I anxiously cried out for a crop failure. That's how intercession tended to go in my life. I prayed, but my prayers often lacked sincerity. My words were more about escaping trouble than communing with God. Entangled in my own foolishness and sin, I didn't get very far in my intercession. I felt clueless about the path forward.

I grew up in church, but fervent prayer wasn't something I encountered very often. Sundays were filled with bowed heads and mumbled prayers, occasionally punctuated by eloquent words that seemed more about impressing an audience than connecting with God. I was trying to go somewhere I had never been, and I didn't know how to get there.

After an awful crisis arose in my family, I knew I had to break out of my old patterns and learn how to pray. Typically, things of the Spirit are only understood after one begins to engage with them. I think most of us who learned how to intercede stumbled our way into the practice.

I knew I had to get there. So I opened my mouth, and it felt terribly awkward. My words meandered aimlessly for a while, but I finally managed to say something heartfelt. In my hour of need, I became honest and raw before the Lord. As my voice trembled, I felt the tremors of the Holy Spirit. Tears streamed down my face as I pleaded with Jesus to come near, and His mercy enveloped me.

I came to realize that authentic prayer isn't about polished phrases; it's about baring one's soul before God. I was struck by the words of Samuel Chadwick, a gifted Methodist intercessor who said, "Prayer is not a collection of balanced phrases; it is the pouring out of the soul. What is love if it be not fiery? What are prayers if the heart be not ablaze?"[1]

Earnest prayer changes hearts and opens the door to some wonderful things. If you want to prevail in the face of weakness, failure, and disappointment, turn to heartfelt prayer. This posture positions you to move closer to the Lord.

Crying Out to the Lord

In the tumultuous times of the judges, Israel stood on the edge of calamity. The Midianites, joining forces with nomads from nearby nations, unleashed havoc on the land. Swarming like locusts, these formidable men devoured the crops—leaving the Valley of Jezreel in desolation (see Judges 6:1–6). Israel teetered on the brink of destruction, and the stakes couldn't have been higher.

The Midianites and their allies didn't just stop at decimating Israel's grain; they unsheathed their swords against the sheep, cattle, and donkeys. They "invaded the land to ravage it" (Judges 6:5 NIV). Bewildered and desperate, the people fled to the hills, seeking refuge in caverns as waves of camel-riding marauders descended. The very survival of Israel hung in the balance, and the future looked bleak.

Times of turmoil force individuals to reassess life. When faced with adversity, people's priorities inevitably shift. Trouble forces believers to cast aside distractions and return to what matters.

As Israel teetered on the edge of starvation, families felt urgency to get help from the Lord. In the face of adversity, prayer is a lifeline. Scripture vividly captures this moment, stating: "Midian so impoverished the Israelites that they cried out to the LORD for help" (Judges 6:6 NIV).

Many prayers are superficial, but even the smallest steps toward God are commendable. In the context of Israel's situation, the people's prayers stemmed more from desperation than genuine repentance. All other options had failed, so they turned to the Lord for refuge.

It's truly a blessing that God extended His mercy so generously to Israel—and to us as well. Though our prayers may not always spring from the deepest wells of sincerity, the Lord often reshapes our words, leading us toward a more profound connection with Him.

When the Israelites cried out as they faced their political, social, and economic setbacks, it marked the beginning of their deliverance. The cries of God's people have the potential to unlock remarkable transformations. Prayer releases so many beautiful things.

Does Prayer Make a Difference?

I had a conversation with a businessman who was grappling with the challenges of rising costs and a shrinking market share. The looming threat of bankruptcy had cast a long shadow over him, leaving him anxious about the future.

Amid the chaotic rhythms of managing his business, he realized he had been neglecting a crucial aspect of his life: his connection with God. The relentless grind of his day-to-day operations had taken precedence over what truly mattered.

Reassuring him about God's compassion, I made it clear that the sincere prayers of believers never fall on deaf ears. Despite any missteps a person may have taken, heartfelt prayers have the power to pave the way for a turnaround. Spirit-led intercession always carries a spark of hope.

In our dialogue, I shared stories of individuals who, like him, sought divine intervention amid tumultuous events. One such instance was during the financial Panic of 1857. As banks shuttered and businesses floundered, a sense of fear gripped America. Overnight, money became scarce, and suspicions arose.

Amid this turmoil, Jeremiah Lanphier, a pastor situated near New York's bustling financial center, made a courageous decision. He extended an invitation to businessmen to join him for a noontime prayer gathering. Initially the attendance was modest, with only six participants, but the meetings gained momentum with time. Soon other congregations and meeting halls opened their doors midday—drawing thousands to engage in earnest intercession.

These prayers, astonishingly, not only played a crucial role in stabilizing the economy, but also helped fan the flames of a glorious revival. The historical records from 1857 to 1859 bear witness to the astonishing fact that as many as one million people made commitments to follow Jesus during this stretch. That's quite astounding at a time when America had only thirty-one million people.

Throughout history, prayer has played a vital role in the advance of God's Kingdom. In fact, it would be a challenging task to pinpoint any move of God that didn't have intercessors diligently praying. A. T. Pierson, a beloved evangelist, recognized this, saying, "There has never been a spiritual awakening in any country or locality that did not begin in united prayer."[2]

Defining Prayer

What is the meaning of prayer? I've found that people tend to forget what it truly means. It is important to recall the things that hold genuine significance. I think that's part of the reason why Scripture talks so much about remembrance. Peter says, "I will always remind you of these things, even though you know them and are firmly established in the truth you now have. I think it is right to refresh your memory" (2 Peter 1:12–13 NIV).

I've observed that intercession, particularly the kind that catalyzes change, originates in the depths of the heart. It finds its external expression as it wells up from within. It can be likened to a sincere and impassioned human cry that harmonizes with the frequencies of heaven.

Intercession often serves as the conduit bridging the earthly realm to the throne room of God. It is more than mere words; it is dialogue that reestablishes intimacy and alignment. Prayer enables us to see things from a higher plane and respond with the heart of the Lord.

Praying heartfelt prayers gives believers a profound opportunity to establish a connection with the Father. We get to share the same kind of intimate relationship that Jesus enjoyed during His earthly ministry in the first century. He once said,

Don't you believe that I am in the Father, and that the Father is in me? The words I say to you I do not speak on my own authority. Rather, it is the Father, living in me, who is doing his work. Believe me when I say that I am in the Father and the Father is in me.

John 14:10–11 NIV

Jesus communed with the heavenly Father daily, walking with Him and talking with Him. This set a compelling example for all His followers to emulate. Beyond mere words, prayer is a sincere cry that unlocks the door to the goodness and mercy of the Lord. It opens the door to the glories of heaven.

Why Prayer Gets Overlooked

Misconceptions persist in the Body of Christ about prayer. Many believe that only a select few can enter into the deeper places with God. They perceive it as a skill reserved for a privileged minority, but this simply isn't true.

Recently, I had a conversation with someone who mentioned having plans to travel and receive prayer from an internationally recognized evangelist. The person highlighted the supposed anointing this evangelist carried. It's undeniable that some have cultivated an intimacy with the Lord and been graced with extraordinary gifts. Nevertheless, there are no actual "superstars" in the expanding Kingdom of God. Why have the obsessions with celebrity that we see in the broader culture entered the Church?

The modern Spirit-filled movement grapples with a troubling trend: a pursuit of wealth and status. These pursuits nearly always lead to the neglect of prayer. Instead of lifting our own voices in intercession, we often wait for someone who is presumed to possess a "greater anointing" to pray on our behalf. This mirrors the distorted values of the church at Corinth. Paul rebukes them for their divisive affiliations, saying, "One of you says, 'I follow

Paul'; another, 'I follow Apollos'; another, 'I follow Cephas'; still another, 'I follow Christ'" (1 Corinthians 1:12 NIV). If we want prayers to arise, we need to get over this "factious spirit,"[3] with all its selfishness and self-promotion.

Not only do we often lean on spiritual celebrities to carry the burden of prayer, but we also want them to give us new revelations. I once encountered a man carrying a sizable notebook brimming with highlighted reflections. He said, "Hit me up with me some fresh manna, Preacher!" Many aren't interceding because they enjoy "being fooled by fancy talk" (Colossians 2:4 CEV).

Instead of being swayed by empty "prophetic" phrases or seemingly impressive credentials, we need to get back to carrying the burden of prayer for ourselves. Every believer possesses the capacity for heartfelt intercession.

A lot of religious posturing gets silly. People make a lot over very little. Effective prayer is not about adding more; it's often about removing unnecessary things. Life-changing intercession draws near to the Spirit of God, casting off fleshly concerns. One of the great intercessors in history, Gerhard Tersteegen, summed it up like this:

> You are the child of God. God's nature is in you. It has only become overclouded. Withdraw from outward things. Pray, and you will make contact again with God, the source of your being. Forget yourself. Forget your selfish desires. Look to God. Die to your own will, live for God's will and you will know true life.[4]

The kind of intercession I'm talking about is not about being loud or uttering perfect words. It's about being immersed in the thoughts and plans of God—partnering with Him in His mission to redeem the world.

Corey Russell, a dear friend of mine, said, "Intercession is God's brilliant strategy for including the saints in ruling with

Him in power. Its mystery is in its weakness, simplicity, humility, and accessibility to all."[5] Prayer helps us align with the order and purposes of heaven. It's how believers walk in authority.

Not Just Prayer, but Action

In Gideon's time, there was a pressing need to learn how to pray and align with the ways of God. This is also a need today. Heartfelt, Spirit-led prayer remains vital. Yet even more is required from believers. We must also be prepared to act.

During a conversation with an "intercessory missionary" who was praying for the Gospel to spread in the Middle East, I encouraged him to participate in a short-term mission trip. He waved off my suggestion, reiterating that his calling was to prayer alone. While I respect his intentions, I find it difficult to believe that only a handful are called to go on mission, while thousands are to remain in prayer rooms.

We find a similar breakdown in the first century. King Herod apprehended Peter, with the goal of executing him. This naturally aroused concern among believers, and they began interceding. Nevertheless, when the angel broke Peter out of prison, the Christians were so preoccupied with their intercession that they didn't open the front door:

> [Peter] went to the home of Mary, the mother of John Mark, where many were gathered for prayer. He knocked at the door in the gate, and a servant girl named Rhoda came to open it. When she recognized Peter's voice, she was so overjoyed that, instead of opening the door, she ran back inside and told everyone, "Peter is standing at the door!"
>
> "You're out of your mind!" they said. . . .
>
> Meanwhile, Peter continued knocking. When they finally opened the door and saw him, they were amazed.
>
> Acts 12:12–16 NLT

This story illustrates a common problem: Some people are so consumed with prayer that they neglect the practical aspects of carrying out God's will. While intercession is vital, it must be accompanied by bold action. You and I cannot sit idly by while the Lord is calling us to be His hands and His feet. Paul wanted to remind us that "we are fellow workmen (joint promoters, laborers together) with *and* for God" (1 Corinthians 3:9 AMPC).

As believers, we must not only pray for God's will to be done; we must also be willing to let Him use us to accomplish it. We need to be prayerful and proactive. Believing and acting on what the Lord has revealed is as important as the words you speak. Twentieth-century firebrand A. W. Tozer said,

> It is useless for large companies of believers to spend long hours begging God to send revival. Unless we intend to reform we may as well not pray. Unless praying men have the insight and faith to amend their whole way of life to conform to the New Testament pattern there can be no true revival.[6]

Heartfelt, Spirit-led prayer should spur one to action. Words alone will never get the job done.

More Than Lips and Fingertips

As the Spirit draws near, prayer surges. The fervent supplications of the faithful serve as an unmistakable sign of the Lord's presence. People sometimes ask, Is prayer a prerequisite for a move of God, or merely the herald of it already in motion? I don't know—perhaps it's a little of both.

Throughout the annals of history, outpourings of the Holy Spirit have always had direct ties to the intercession of saints. Devout individuals have been called upon to partner with the Holy Spirit—conducting heartfelt prayer in living rooms, businesses, and every realm of life. These men and women are agents of reconciliation to a broken world. Samuel Chadwick said, "The prayer that prevails is not the work of lips and fingertips. It is the cry of a broken heart."[7]

Prevailing prayer transcends all our words and actions, emanating from a heart filled with God's love. Jesus undoubtedly had all of this in mind when He said, "Out of the overflow of the heart, the mouth speaks" (Luke 6:45 BSB).

4

IN THE WINEPRESS

God Meets You Where You Are

▌ J. D. KING

Difficult circumstances can make life hard. During the tough seasons, it's natural to feel like God is distant. If you take a closer look, however, you will see that He frequently enters the rough places alongside us—comforting and sustaining us. From personal experience, I have discovered that God meets us right where we are.

My wife and I were eager to start a family after we got married. With Bobbie's affinity for children, it was no surprise that we made this decision. On Sunday mornings, if you walk into our church, you will probably find an infant on her lap and a toddler tugging on her pant leg. All the kids light up when they are around Bobbie.

Nevertheless, starting a family wasn't as easy as we imagined. Despite our friends' reassurances that God would make it happen, we encountered setbacks, and months went by without any indication that we would become parents. We sought medical help, and the doctors discovered that Bobbie had endometriosis, a painful affliction where tissue grows outside the uterus—obstructing the fallopian tubes. Bobbie had a particularly severe case, and things weren't looking good.

We scheduled a surgery to remove Bobbie's excess tissue, and she began taking Clomid, a medicine that assists with ovulation. Later we also tried intrauterine insemination, a technique that enhances the chance of fertilization. But none of these procedures worked. We had spent a lot of money and were still childless.

After Bobbie underwent several more invasive medical tests, the doctor summoned us to his office and delivered the devastating news: "I'm sorry, but there are no further treatments I can offer."

The words hit me hard, and I began trembling with a sense of uncertainty. The wound cut even deeper as I saw tears well up in my wife's eyes. The pain etched on her face was heart-wrenching. Bobbie possessed a nurturing spirit, and the thought of being unable to have children was unbearable. Our infertility was a burden we didn't know how to handle.

No matter the odds, it's important to keep fighting for a breakthrough. Trust in the marvelous grace of God. Even when you're scraping the bottom, and it seems nothing can rectify the situation, there is still hope. The Father of lights still shows up in the dark places.

Amid the shadows and despair, Bobbie found herself on her knees, her anguished cries reaching up to the heavens. I couldn't help but join her in her travail. Our cheeks were awash with torrents of tears that began pooling on the floor. The pursuit of a miracle generally isn't a picturesque affair, but desperate people aren't concerned about appearances.

Bobbie and I entered into a time of soul-searching and prayer. While we were grieving and trying to figure out our next step, however, the Holy Spirit continued to comfort us. It made a world of difference to know that we weren't alone.

One night a few months later, Bobbie responded to the stirrings of the Holy Spirit. She began crawling on her knees—reaching out to the Lord in fervent intercession. In many ways, my wife was like the woman with the issue of blood in the Gospels. She wasn't going to let Jesus pass her by (see Luke 8:43–48).

The love of the Lord is mind-blowing. Just when it seemed as if all hope was lost, God intervened and brought forth the impossible. A miracle ensued, and nine months later we were blessed with the birth of our precious daughter, Allyson Grace.

Let me tell you, God can step into the darkest places and turn bad situations around. He has done this for my family, and I believe He can do it for you as well. I've been delighted to find that mercy and grace keep showing up in the most unexpected places.

Things don't always go the way we hope, and sometimes things can, in fact, fall apart. But the Lord steps into these places with us and helps us find our way. It's important to remember that revival doesn't usually begin in a place of triumph; it begins in the place of brokenness and pain.

Hiding in the Winepress

During the time of Gideon, the nation of Israel experienced a severe crisis as hordes of Midianites invaded their borders. Over a grueling span of seven years, the bloodthirsty raiders wreaked havoc, devastating livestock and plundering grain. These attacks plunged God's people into a state of turmoil and instability.

Amid the chaos, Gideon, from the tribe of Manasseh, emerged as a pivotal voice. Despite feeling as though he came from the most insignificant family in the weakest Israeli clan (see Judges 6:15), something had to be done. He gathered whatever meager harvest he could salvage to thresh and carried it to "the bottom of a winepress to hide the grain from the Midianites" (Judges 6:11 NLT).

Winepresses of the time were hewn from stone and strategically located in secluded spots, hidden from plain view. In contrast, threshing floors, where grains were processed, were completely exposed atop windswept hills. Gideon's decision to thresh his grain in the winepress not only allowed him to stay undetected, but also safeguarded his meager possessions.

Gideon was resourceful, but it was still dehumanizing to have to hide in his own backyard. He knew it wasn't God's heart for the Israelites to scurry around like rats in the darkness—fighting for a few morsels of food. The righteous ones are destined to triumph, not to be under the thumb of foreign invaders.

Many believers expect God to intervene in this world, but they believe it will happen in big, audacious spaces rather than in quiet, hidden corners. Churchgoers expect the Lord to ascend to the top of the mountain rather than descend into the depths of the valley. Yet the winepress is where the angel of the Lord met Gideon. Unlike us, God is not afraid of the dark.

Understand that on the other side of your crisis are the beauty and wonder of the Lord. Keep pressing in until you see His face.

Light Breaks into the Darkest Night

I've seen God meet with His sons and daughters in the bleakest of nights. No matter how bad it gets, He's never far away. Throughout history, many awakenings have sparked during perilous times. The evangelical statesman Billy Graham once said, "Some of the greatest spiritual revivals in the past occurred just when the situation seemed to be the darkest."[1] God often moves in power when society is almost at a breaking point.

The Second Great Awakening in the United States is a compelling example of this phenomenon. In the early 1800s, pioneers yearned to find freedom in the untamed wilderness. The pioneer men, known for their coarseness, violence, and drinking habits, were independent rationalists who paid little heed to God. Concerns arose that the nation would fall into "Egyptian darkness," following the patterns of the godless libertines in France.

God was not silent, however. Methodist, Baptist, and Presbyterian evangelists braved the untamed frontier, proclaiming the beauty and wonder of Jesus. Some of them organized camp meetings with fervent outdoor preaching. In these gatherings, countless families experienced the overwhelming glory of God. In just a few decades, tens of thousands dedicated their lives to Jesus—leading to radical changes in our nation. Biblical Christianity soon became a defining part of the national consciousness. Even in the darkest times, God can begin to institute beautiful changes.

There are other seasons when the Lord intervened. In the late 1960s, for example, the United States once again found itself grappling with turmoil. Race, gender, and bloodshed in Vietnam ignited a firestorm of anger and unrest. At the same time, the counterculture movement emerging out of California dared to challenge social norms—exacerbating the sense of disillusionment that hung in the air. This period witnessed a widespread rejection of Christian values, resulting in gross immorality and open rebellion. The situation became so dire that some feared for our nation's survival.

Amid the darkness, the Lord began to move, and everything changed. Heavenly glory overtook the hearts of long-haired, unkempt hippies—igniting a marvelous revival. In a remarkably short span of time, thousands of dropouts, drug addicts, and promiscuous youths encountered the life-altering power of the Gospel. The Jesus People movement emerged during an era when most churchgoers had little expectation for anything good. God's plan was not on anyone's calendar, but our nation was rescued once more through a glorious revival.

In the darkest seasons, God appears.

Falling into the Hands of God

Those who have a deep connection with God have learned to trust in His unshakable grace. When life seems to take a wrong turn, they know that the Lord is steadfast. Even during times of suffering and judgment, these faithful ones seek refuge in Him.

King David of Israel sinned and knew that a day of reckoning was coming. Things could have gone several different ways, but he tearfully declared, "Let me fall into the hands of the LORD, for his mercy is very great" (1 Chronicles 21:13 NIV). The king's humble posture touched the Lord's heart. Although the destroyer was positioned to enact judgment, God said, "Enough! Withdraw your hand!" (verse 15 NIV).

David acquired, at full price, the threshing floor of Argunah—the location where this miracle took place. The king offered his sacrifice and "called on the LORD, and the LORD answered him with fire from heaven" (1 Chronicles 21:26 NIV). In a dark, sinful season, the Lord was merciful to David and his countrymen. Israel still experienced judgment, but it wasn't as severe as it could have been.

There are other times in Scripture where we witness seemingly impossible breakthroughs. One such moment occurred during the exodus, when the nation of Israel found itself surrounded by the armies of Egypt. Faced with a dire situation, some of the people grew agitated and started to voice their fears. Moses told them, "Stand still, and see the salvation of the LORD" (Exodus 14:13 NKJV).

With their backs against the wall and seemingly no way out, God intervened, with Moses acting like a conduit: "Moses stretched out his hand over the sea; and the LORD caused the sea to go back" (Exodus 14:21 NKJV). The Israelites walked to safety on dry ground—surrounded by two towering walls of water. These miraculous events serve as a reminder that God shows up in many of the most challenging situations. In the bleakest of nights, a glimmer of light begins to flicker. It happened for them, and it will happen for you too.

God Steps into the Darkness

God's radiant glory shone as Gideon toiled in the winepress. The astonishing turn of events seemed to mirror the words of the prophet Isaiah, who spoke of a heavenly exchange of "beauty for ashes, a joyous blessing instead of mourning" (Isaiah 61:3 NLT). While Gideon was at his lowest point, God orchestrated a profound transformation—positioning a wheat thresher to triumph over his destroyers.

Gideon's experience in the winepress serves as a reminder that heavenly mercies often emerge during challenging seasons. Believers shouldn't be shocked by the fact that the Lord meets us in our moments of disappointment and pain. It's in the darkest nights that His light shines most brilliantly.

I have witnessed a number of remarkable turnarounds over the years. One particularly inspiring story involved a close friend. He had achieved an extraordinary feat—acquiring an insurance agency in his early twenties. Initially he had success, but a tax management mistake threatened to unravel everything he had built.

In the face of this seemingly impossible predicament, my friend turned to the Lord. He and his wife began to intercede and give God generous offerings. My friend recognized that what he had in his wallet wasn't enough to save him. It was time to go all in for the Kingdom of God. Only Jesus could rescue him.

As the deadline for the tax payment drew nearer, an unexpected turn of events transpired. Out of nowhere, my friend received an inheritance that gave him the means to settle the outstanding taxes. It was a breathtaking turnaround, a testament to the Lord's remarkable mercies.

I have witnessed Jesus do things like this repeatedly. He graciously enters our crises. Mercy comes alongside us in our moments of embarrassment and shame. Whenever He comes near, it brings encouragement and a renewed sense of hope.

I recall another situation that took an unexpected turn. I decided to share the Gospel with a waitress. As soon as I mentioned the name of Jesus, however, she became enraged. Without even taking our orders, she turned around and ran off to the back of the restaurant.

Minutes seemed to drag on like hours before she finally returned. Summoning the courage, I extended a heartfelt apology for making her feel uncomfortable. Her response was stern, expressing her desire not to delve any further into the matter. I think every table in the restaurant glared at me. My heart hung heavy in my chest.

Weeks later, I was at a local dog park, and to my astonishment, I found myself face-to-face with the same waitress. This time, her demeanor was different. She approached me with a smile, thanking me for my gracious words at the restaurant that day. Apparently, after our interchange, she recommitted her life to Jesus.

At the time, I couldn't see all that was going on, but once again God brought something good out of a bad situation. When I originally spoke with the waitress, it felt as though everything were broken. I was embarrassed, convinced that I had somehow hindered the Gospel. I couldn't have been more wrong. Jesus brought something beautiful out of the mess.

I have witnessed myriads of people rescued, in the goodness and grace of the Lord, but I don't want to give the impression that Christians never suffer. They often do. I have witnessed once-vibrant marriages end in divorce, and devout believers gasping for their final breaths in a hospital bed. In all of this, however, one thing remains true. The Lord stands beside us and covers us in the winepress. We are never alone.

Whatever you're going through, I'm convinced that God will help you. Adversity is never easy, and it's tempting to lose hope when circumstances don't work out. Nevertheless, I'm confident that the Lord will intervene in your life. He will never leave you nor forsake you.

God's grace operates in mysterious ways and is often quietly at work in the background of your crisis. Although you may not perceive every detail of the Lord's plan, rest assured that He is always present. I encourage you not to let up on your heartfelt intercession. Keep praying passionate prayers. Even in the darkest moments, God has the power to turn things around.

Out of the Winepress

As we navigate challenging seasons, the Lord accompanies us every step of the way. Jesus always goes into the dark places beside us, carrying us through. Scripture makes it clear that He identifies with our suffering and pain (see Hebrews 4:15).

Although God always stands alongside His sons and daughters, He never intended for us to remain in the winepress. Instead, He is beckoning us to step out and embrace our destiny as kingly heirs. Why remain in the pit when we have a glorious inheritance in the Kingdom of God?

David captures the essence of this when he says that God "redeems your life from the pit and crowns you with love and compassion" (Psalm 103:4 NIV). Challenges will inevitably arise, but the Lord never intended for us to linger in the muck and mire. Those who earnestly turn to God are treated as royalty, adorned with His love and tender mercies.

In this hour, many Christians find themselves lulled into complacency by the old, familiar patterns. We can't build a future entirely on where we've been. So it's vital that we keep progressing, moving into the deeper realms of the Kingdom. The apostle Paul said,

> I do not consider myself to have "arrived", spiritually, nor do I consider myself already perfect. But I keep going on, grasping ever more firmly that purpose for which Christ grasped me. My brothers, I do not consider myself to have fully grasped it even now. But I do concentrate on this: I leave the past behind and with hands outstretched to whatever lies ahead I go straight for the goal—my reward the honour of being called by God in Christ.
>
> Philippians 3:12–14 PHILLIPS

Part of moving forward in this season is cultivating a holy dissatisfaction. An old preacher used to say, "Fall in love with mountains, not plateaus." The Bible tells us that we were made to groan inwardly to God—yearning for "our full rights as his adopted children" (Romans 8:23 NLT). It's hard to embrace your glorious destiny in the Kingdom when you are content to live as an orphan.

If you persist in a place of despair, you'll miss out on the breakthrough God intends for you. To get out of the pit, you must be willing to rise. Like Moses on the backside of the desert, you need to be mindful of your destiny and advance with stammering lips. Like most of us, Moses made excuses. He told God, "I get tongue-tied, and my words get tangled" (Exodus 4:10 NLT). But God replied, "Now go! I will be with you as you speak" (verse 12). God is likely saying the same thing to you and me.

I remember an experience I had during prayer a few years ago. While interceding, I found myself visualizing a pair of shoes. As I attempted to slide my feet into them, I was met with an immediate realization: They were far too large. Doubt crept in, and I hesitated, muttering, *Lord, these shoes are too big for me; my feet are too small.* It was in that moment that I felt a gentle response from God: *Put them on, and take a step. You'll grow into them.*

I sensed that God was revealing to me the importance of starting on my journey—even though I felt inadequate and ill-equipped. Transformation and growth often unfold as you progress along the pathway of your destiny. This visceral experience spoke to me—reiterating that I should never remain in a place God didn't intend for me to live.

Amid a dark and fractured world, God releases His goodness and glory. As He steps into the place where you live, His glory supersedes the shadows. God sees you for who you are—warts and all—but He loves you anyway. He is not afraid to enter into brokenness and pain. The vast reach of God's love is unfathomable.

The Lord meets you in the winepress, but He never intended for you to stay there. By His mercy and strength, you are being beckoned to ascend. The story of Gideon serves as a poignant reminder that your starting point should never be your final destination.

5

GOD RAISES UP VOICES

Truth Tellers and World Changers

STEVE GRAY

When God does a mighty work on the earth, He raises up people who will speak on His behalf. They become His mouthpieces and serve as channels for His will to be done at a certain time, in a certain place—including where you are right now. This is His pattern throughout the Bible and throughout human history. Gideon was one of those voices, and—amazingly—you and I are called to be voices too.

In Gideon's day, the Israelites had suffered for seven long years under the grinding heels of their enemies, and when they cried out to the Lord, He sent them a voice in the form of a prophet who told them,

> This is what the Lord, the God of Israel, says: I brought you up out of slavery in Egypt. I rescued you from the Egyptians and from

all who oppressed you. I drove out your enemies and gave you their land. I told you, "I am the LORD your God. You must not worship the gods of the Amorites, in whose land you now live." But you have not listened to me.

Judges 6:8–10 NLT

That was voice number one. Then a second voice spoke, that of an angel of the Lord who visited Gideon at a winepress. There, the angel and Gideon had a life-changing—and history-changing—conversation: "When the angel of the LORD appeared to Gideon, he said, 'The LORD is with you, mighty warrior'" (Judges 6:12 NIV). Then the Lord declared to him: "Go in the strength you have and save Israel out of Midian's hand. Am I not sending you?" (verse 14).

I have often heard well-meaning Bible teachers portray Gideon as a coward hiding in a winepress, but I don't see him that way. I perceive him as clever and determined to be a provider in the worst circumstances. I see in him tenacity and ingenuity, not fear. That said, when the angel addressed him as "mighty warrior," Gideon seemed not to understand God's view of him. He responded as most of us probably would, by declaring himself the weakest and least. But the angel of the Lord appeared specifically to him, and this was no mistake. The angel didn't check his notes and realize he had gone to the wrong address. No, it was time for a nation's deliverance, and God had decided it was up to Gideon, a new voice, to put His plan into action.

God handpicked Gideon, just as He handpicks you and me for specific works. He observed something in Gideon that He Himself had put there—the mettle of a mighty warrior who would release Israel from her oppressors' grip. Raised up by God, Gideon was about to speak for a nation. We, too, are meant to be the voice of God in our circumstances. Paul called these assignments "every good work" and said that God planned them in advance for us to do. We must take those words seriously.

Yet, like Gideon, many of us don't see ourselves as God does. We claim to be the weakest and least, often in the name of humility. We talk ourselves down and profess not to have the strength to be God's voice in our situations. But also like Gideon, we don't need more strength; we just need a "yes." Gideon was able to conquer with the strength he already possessed. In the same way, as weak and least as we may feel, all God requires is that we have the faith to believe that His prevailing strength can work through us.

God wants to do amazing feats on this earth, using people just like you. He is calling men and women to rise from the winepresses of toil and rally nations to do great exploits. Your voice is one God wants to use to accomplish a work of eternal value somewhere on this earth. You and I don't have the right to underestimate ourselves any more than Gideon did. When God speaks and calls us "mighty warriors," our job is to take Him at His word, rise from the invisible place, and trust the Lord that we already possess the strength to do what He is calling us to do.

The Gideon in Me

I can identify somewhat with Gideon. My father died at the age of forty-seven. It was a tragic loss, not only for our family personally, but for our finances. He had been our only source of income. Now, money and food were hard to come by. Like Gideon working in the winepress, I had to come up with schemes to get by. So, every year I became a carny and worked at the State Fair. The carnival was a tough place to work—very different from today's theme parks, where young employees are well-dressed and well-treated. I was the teenage worker with holes in his jeans who spent hours a day asking people to "step right up and try your luck." My bosses also made me carry a heavy wooden ladder and hang banners on the highest part of the stadium. It was dangerous grunt work that no one else wanted to do.

One summer I also worked at a country club, starting my days early to do things like clean the pool. The pool water was always cold, and I never knew what I would find there. One morning, there was an entire tractor in the deep end. Who was going to get it out and clean up that oily mess? You guessed it: me.

My other job was at the local farmers' supply store, where I assembled two-story grain silos in hundred-degree heat. When I finished one, I was stuck inside with my brains virtually boiling, until someone brought a ladder so I could climb out and start on another silo. I did all of this for a dollar an hour. At times, the job seemed to be a metaphor for my entire life: stuck in a stifling silo with no hope of ever getting out. Maybe you've felt that way, as if you were spending your life and efforts on unimportant issues. Maybe, like Gideon, you've concluded that you don't have what it takes to make a difference in this world. That was certainly how I felt with no father to help me find my way and succeed. How could I ever become anything more than a carny or a day laborer?

I don't believe Gideon ever dreamed that an angel would come along and change his life, but that's what happened. In a similar way, I never imagined that God would take notice of me, but He did. My journey toward His purposes began when I was six years old, at the Nazarene church my family attended. One day, my dad and the pastor found me kneeling at the altar and sobbing in the empty sanctuary. They were amazed when I declared, "I've been called to preach."

If you are a mother or father, please don't underestimate the power of God as it relates to your children. He can and does call them into intimate, effective, and powerful relationships at young ages. I am proof of that.

The only problem with my epiphany was that I forgot about it for the next seventeen years. But when I was twenty-three, God surprised me again, saving me by His mercy and baptizing me in the Holy Spirit. I sang in the Spirit, magnified the Lord, and then declared, "I've been called to preach," just as I had when I was a boy. But this time, like Gideon, I emerged from my winepress ready to speak the will of God to my generation—or at least to anyone who would listen.

The Strong and the Weak

It's not just the weakest or least God calls to be a voice. Sometimes He uses people of apparently great strength.

For example, Paul, a great theologian, became the voice of the Gospel to the Gentiles. In doing so, he took a journey from seeing himself as the greatest to glorying in his weakness. When Paul pleaded for relief from his thorn in the flesh, God said to him, "My grace is sufficient for you, for my power is made perfect in weakness" (2 Corinthians 12:9 NIV). Like Gideon, Paul was discovering that God's power shines brightest and works strongest in weakness. God was offering to Paul what He had offered to Gideon. The Lord had told Gideon, "Go in the strength you have." The message to Paul was that the grace he already had from God was sufficient for the tasks.

Most Christians are well aware that grace is unmerited favor—but grace is much more than that. It is empowerment we would not otherwise have. Religion likes to emphasize the fact that we are undeserving, but I think God would rather we appreciate and celebrate the power of God that is ours. Grace empowers us to be what we cannot be on our own, to do what we cannot do on our own, and to go where we cannot go on our own. As we grow to count on His grace, we find it is all-sufficient for us, just as it was for Paul and Gideon. By His grace, we can be His voices—if we are willing to say "yes" and go in the strength we already have.

Brave Leaders, Strong Voices

Gideon became a military leader the moment the Spirit of the Lord came upon him: "Then the Spirit of the LORD came on Gideon, and he blew a trumpet, summoning the Abiezrites to follow him" (Judges 6:34 NIV). His trumpet became his voice to summon troops from his clan and surrounding Israelite families. Because of his faith, courage, and obedience, he was able to call 32,000 men to follow him against the vast army set on destroying them. What an amazing example of going in the strength you have.

The world today needs bold leaders whose strong, clear voices resound like Gideon's trumpet. His message called people to return to the Lord and defeat the enemy. Today, no less than in Gideon's day, we need leaders courageous enough to tell us to return to the Lord and forsake the idols of this world, so we can be delivered from demonic oppressors that breed division, chaos, and destruction.

Powers of darkness swarm like armies, building up encampments from which to wage war on humanity. You and I, our families, our livelihoods, our communities, and our churches are all in their sights.

Will you be a clarion voice? Will you go in the strength that you have, to rout these enemies?

Heroic Voices

The Bible tells of many heroes who passed tests like Gideon's. These people, destined to become voices for God, endured many hardships that tried their faith and honed their spiritual skills. It took Moses eighty years to become the voice of deliverance chosen to lead the Israelites out of slavery in Egypt. Despite his initial reluctance, Moses emerged as a powerful voice for God, boldly confronting Pharaoh and leading the Israelites to freedom through the Red Sea—all in spite of his perceived weaknesses.

David, anointed by God to be king of Israel, began as a lowly shepherd singing psalms of praise and victory as he tended his sheep. When Goliath brought shame on Israel, David's voice rose up, shouting, "Who is this uncircumcised Philistine that he should defy the armies of the living God?" (1 Samuel 17:26 NIV). He not only killed Goliath, but also rallied Israel's army to defeat the Philistine armies.

The prophet Elijah stood up against the wickedness of King Ahab and Queen Jezebel and boldly proclaimed God's truth to the people. He challenged Israel, "If the LORD is God, follow him" (1 Kings 18:21 NIV). Sadly, the children of Israel could not even open their mouths! It was his voice that called down fire from heaven to demonstrate God's power and authority. Yet Elijah, the book of James tells us, was nothing more or less than "a man with a nature like ours" (James 5:17 NKJV).

Jesus is the ultimate example of a person God raised up to speak on His behalf. "I only say what my Father says, and I only do what my Father does," He confessed (see John 5:19; 12:49). Jesus performed countless miracles, healed the sick, and preached the message of God's love and salvation to all who would listen, and He did it in the power of the Father's grace alone.

In world history, God always chooses courageous people to be His mouthpieces—ordinary people like William Wilberforce, who fought for the abolition of slavery, and Mother Teresa, who dedicated her life to serving the poor and marginalized. Other voices like George Whitefield, John Wesley, and Jonathan Edwards preached revivals that broke denominational boundaries and set hearts ablaze for God, resulting in society-shifting great awakenings.

As we study these heroes, we see a biblical pattern of how voices are raised up. First, the people of God find themselves under the thumb of their enemies. They begin to cry out to God for rescue. God hears their cries and calls forth a leader to serve as the messenger of deliverance. The chosen messenger must pass tests of character, faith, and obedience. Then, that person begins to speak God's message and instructions to obtain deliverance for the people. Finally, the people follow his or her lead into battle, and victory is won.

I believe many heroes are waiting in the wings. You can become one of them, if you are willing to walk the path of preparation in the strength God provides, which is always enough.

The Message of God's Voices

In Gideon's day, Elijah's day, Paul's day, or our own day, God's voices—His prophets—only have one message. It's the same word for every nation, community, region, synagogue, and church. The prophet preceding Gideon brought this specific truth: God had brought the nation out of slavery and delivered them from their oppressors. He warned them not to worship other gods in the land where they lived, but they didn't listen. Now they were being ransacked by foreign nations.

Jesus preached the message: "Repent, for the Kingdom of God is near." Whatever He spoke about in all His parables and teaching, the core of His message was always the same: Turn from this world to the Kingdom of God, which is now here.

It was the same message Jonah gave to everybody in the region of Nineveh. In essence, "Repent, and bad things won't happen to you. If you don't repent, disaster lies ahead."

This was also the basic message of Peter, and Paul, and every messenger God sent. God's voices have one main message that applies to everyone: *Turn from the kingdom of this world to the Kingdom of God.*

You Can Be a Voice

God has created you to be a voice. Have you ever desired to say something meaningful to a friend in need, beyond something sympathetic and trite? Why not ask God to speak through you to bring divine help? He has appointed all believers to flow in the river of His "gifts of the [Holy] Spirit," as listed in 1 Corinthians 12:1, 7–11 (NIV). These gifts are supernatural manifestations of God's Spirit through believers, and they empower each of us to be a voice for Him. They reveal God's heart for the hearers at that moment, and they come forth for the good of all.

Because of these gifts, including the word of wisdom, the word of knowledge, and the gift of prophecy, you and I can speak to a friend for his or her strengthening, encouragement, and comfort. You can take a step of faith to move in the power of the Holy Spirit and speak for God. As you do, you will "hear" a word or two in your spirit. As you speak those words, more life-giving words will flow from your mouth.

If you dream of becoming a voice for God, able to be fruitful in these important times, here are simple steps you can take to put yourself in a position to be used:

- Develop your message by studying God's Word and hearing yourself speak it aloud.
- Begin by being a voice right where you are. Your spouse and children will benefit by hearing you speak God's heart for your family.
- If you are faithful in little things, God will give you more and greater things. You won't get to speak to the church, government officials, or world rulers before you practice speaking life, encouragement, and truth in your day-to-day life.
- Don't disqualify yourself! Never tell yourself that you are too young, too old, untrained, fearful, or shy to talk to friends, strangers, or groups.
- "See" yourself speaking God's wisdom to everyone, everywhere, with confidence, authority, and anointing. Say yes to His vision for you.
- Take every opportunity to be that voice for God and speak up!

As you put your voice to use, you will be part of the unfolding of God's end-times plan. That may sound overly grand, but Jesus said in Matthew 24:14 (NIV), "And this gospel of the kingdom will be preached in the whole world as a testimony to all nations, and then the end will come." The end comes by voices. It doesn't come by disasters or wars, earthquakes, floods, hurricanes, or tornadoes.

It comes through preaching. God raises up voices to end this age and begin the new one. This is why John the Baptist, when asked who he was, answered, "I am a voice . . ." (John 1:23 NLT).

You, too, are a voice. So am I. All believers, collectively, are the voice of the will of God in the earth. It is time to say yes to the ministry of your voice. Matthew 10:27 (NLT) says, "What I whisper in your ear, shout from the housetops for all to hear!" Let those words summon you to the battlefront, just as the trumpet sounded forth in Gideon's army, signaling the sure victory that was to come.

6

RATTLING BONES AND SMALL CLOUDS

Find What God Is Doing and Run with It

J. D. KING

Most people think they are ready for what God is doing, but that's rarely the case. I went off to Bible school hoping to encounter the Lord, but I couldn't find Him there. Truthfully, my classmates and I weren't ready to come face-to-face with the glory. It's one thing to read about it on a page, but something else to encounter it firsthand. As ministry students, we thought we were fiery and uncompromising, but a religious spirit was taming us and stealing our fervor.

When I entered my second year at Central Bible College in Springfield, Missouri, theology gripped me more than spirituality. I didn't know it, but I was on the wrong trajectory. Something unsettling had seized me, and I didn't recognize it.

I thought I had things figured out. Consequently, when I heard testimonies about what God was doing around the globe, I was bothered. The spiritual intensity in these groups felt like a threat to my status. If their outlook was right, I was missing something. Honestly, I didn't like that notion at all.

Whether I preferred it or not, revival was ablaze in the mid-1990s. Crowds were traveling to hot spots in North America and Europe. Many spiritually dry people were experiencing fresh touches from God. The Lord was at work, and I didn't see it at all.

Shortly after the revival began in Smithton, I began attending the services. I joined thousands who were journeying to this outpouring only two hours from my college. One night, I made my way to the front. I wasn't sure what I was doing. I had already given my life to Jesus and was baptized in the Holy Spirit. As the waves of God's presence washed over me, however, I found myself in one of the most intense spiritual battles I had ever faced. A metamorphosis is seldom pretty.

In my spirit, I finally recognized that the hand of the Lord was at work, but the struggle intensified. I cried out, *Lord, why is there a disconnect? Why can't I receive something blessed by You?*

As I basked in the Lord's presence, it became clear that my pride and desire for control were holding me back. I had more faith in my formulated doctrines than in the stirrings of the Holy Spirit. Even as I recognized the Lord at work, it was still a battle to give myself entirely over to Him.

Jesus has a way of smashing our idols—particularly of the religious variety. He breaks in and transforms everything. As I bathed in the radiant glow of my "Damascus Road" experience, I was aware that it would alter the course of my life. I once heard someone say there are eighteen inches between heaven and hell—the distance from your head to your heart. In my case, this axiom couldn't have been more accurate.

I didn't understand everything going on, but I was finally willing to press into the great unknown. That night, a raging fire was lit in my soul, and all these years later, it still hasn't gone out.

A Realization

God moves in mysterious ways, and it can be difficult to recognize all He's doing. This truth is exemplified in Gideon's story. While Gideon was threshing grain in the winepress, an angel appeared and said, "The LORD is with you, mighty warrior" (Judges 6:12 NIV).

Initially, this wheat thresher didn't realize he was speaking to a heavenly messenger. Gideon foolishly declared: "If the LORD is with us, why has all this happened to us? Where are all his wonders that our ancestors told us about when they said, 'Did not the LORD bring us up out of Egypt?' But now the LORD has abandoned us" (Judges 6:13 NIV).

Gideon's comments revealed a lack of spiritual awareness. He second-guessed God and even had the nerve to suggest that the Lord had abandoned Israel. These are not the kind of words you would expect from one God is raising up.

Fortunately, as the conversation continued, Gideon sensed that something profound was taking place. He asked this mysterious figure to wait while he stepped away to prepare an offering. A little later, when Gideon presented the food,

> The angel of the LORD touched the meat and bread with the tip of the staff in his hand, and fire flamed up from the rock and consumed all he had brought. And the angel of the LORD disappeared.
>
> When Gideon realized that it was the angel of the LORD, he cried out.
>
> Judges 6:21–22 NLT

As the angel released holy fire that consumed the sacrifice, Gideon realized that he had been standing near heavenly splendor all along. He finally comprehended realities that he had failed to see before.

Like Gideon, believers may not always recognize the Lord's presence in and around them. The wind may shift, and bones may rattle, but not everyone is attuned to what the Spirit is doing. It's essential to remain open to the presence of the Lord, even when His works are not immediately apparent.

We need the Lord to open the eyes of our hearts.

Jesus, Help Us See!

I once knew a man named David who led a small group. Some of the people he was leading had powerful spiritual encounters on their own. A few of his group members were baptized in the Holy Spirit and spoke in tongues.

David, who was non-charismatic at the time, didn't think this was a valid experience, and he sidelined those who were desiring more of God. Their leader's attitude was confusing to the group. Even those who hadn't had the same experiences felt as though David was too stringent.

In one of the subsequent gatherings, a member asked everyone to pray for his struggling teenager. Intercession erupted in the room. The voices grew more intense, and within moments the group was praying for some other needs. Everyone in that room could feel the stirrings of the Holy Spirit.

As all of this was going on, David stepped over to the corner, away from the group. The prayers rose for a while, but then the voices faded. Finally, there was silence, and everyone turned to David to see what he wanted to do next. Their leader, however, remained silent.

Then all at once, David started speaking in tongues. In a matter of moments, God disrupted this introverted leader's world. The very thing he was dismissive of came upon him. The glory of the Lord enveloped him.

Afterward, David and the entire group were able to grow in things of the Spirit—side by side. It took him some time, but this group leader finally recognized the hand of God at work. Sometimes Christians miss what the Lord is up to in the world. Without eyes to see, you will never recognize the hand of God. Jesus, help us see!

Can You Hear the Rumblings?

Throughout the Bible, God was often moving before the masses recognized it. In one instance, the prophet Ezekiel encountered a prelude to a marvelous work. He heard rattling bones. At first, it was merely a rumbling, not a manifestation. Not every believer can see where things are going. Can you?

Ezekiel prophesied, and as he spoke, the noise of the bones coming together grew louder, until they joined bone to bone: "So I prophesied as I was commanded. And as I was prophesying, there was a noise, a rattling sound, and the bones came together, bone to bone" (Ezekiel 37:7 NIV).

Finally, after the fragments came together, the breath of the Lord entered the lifeless bodies. That which was dead was rejuvenated. Some believers can peer behind the veil. They can see what's happening around them. Nevertheless, not everyone can do this. Can you?

In Scripture, we find other examples of these rumblings. We could also look to the story of Elijah. During a severe drought, this prophet heard the sound of rain, signaling the coming of refreshment and renewal. He sensed that this was a sign of heavenly intervention. It was time to start looking for the cloud, even if it was small:

> Elijah said to Ahab, ". . . there is the sound of a heavy rain." . . . Elijah climbed to the top of Carmel, bent down to the ground and put his face between his knees.

"Go and look toward the sea," he told his servant. And he went up and looked.

"There is nothing there," he said.

Seven times Elijah said, "Go back."

The seventh time the servant reported, "A cloud as small as a man's hand is rising from the sea."

So Elijah said, "Go and tell Ahab, 'Hitch up your chariot and go down before the rain stops you.'"

Meanwhile, the sky grew black with clouds, the wind rose, a heavy rain started falling and Ahab rode off to Jezreel.

1 Kings 18:41–45 NIV

Significant events often emerge from unassuming origins. Take, for example, the rainstorm that ended this long-standing drought. It was initiated by a minuscule cloud. While many ignore the potential of seemingly insignificant occurrences, those with keen spiritual eyes can discern where things are going.

Every move of God has a starting point, which often goes unnoticed by many. People may assume that revival begins as a raging river, but this is not usually the case. In reality, an outpouring often begins as a small trickle. This concept is so misunderstood that the prophet Zechariah declared, "Who dares despise the day of small things?" (Zechariah 4:10 NIV). Don't discount seemingly small beginnings.

Just as a raging fire is sparked by a few small embers, the birth of a soul-stirring revival can also emerge subtly. That's what happened in Smithton, Missouri. When the outpouring began, it probably didn't look impressive to outsiders. They might have even questioned whether it was even a revival. Nevertheless, the people discerned that a flame had been lit. They felt a calling from the Lord to nurture and protect the fire. These individuals knew that they needed to be vigilant because the Lord was present in a special way.

Every raging fire begins with a few small sparks.

Missing Your Time of Visitation

When it comes to matters of the Kingdom, we don't always have the right outlook. Many believe that when God moves, it will be recognized and received by the masses. Yet that seldom happens. The sad truth is that many Christians remain indifferent about spiritual matters.

Spiritual insensitivity has been a recurring issue throughout history. God's people have often been "stiff-necked" and "unyielding." The prophet Zechariah warned Israel about repeating their ancestors' mistake of ignoring prophetic warnings, but the masses didn't listen (see Zechariah 1:4).

Later, in the first century, Jesus was deeply troubled by the spiritual blindness in Jerusalem. He warned the people that they were on the verge of missing a holy visitation. Jesus lamented, "If you had known, even you, especially in this your day, the things that make for your peace! But now they are hidden from your eyes. . . . you did not know the time of your visitation" (Luke 19:42, 44 NKJV).

In the book of Acts, Stephen was brought before the Sanhedrin, and he boldly preached to those gatekeepers of Jerusalem. He declared, "You stiff-necked and uncircumcised in heart and ears! You always resist the Holy Spirit; as your fathers did, so do you" (Acts 7:51 NKJV).

While contemporary Christians may believe that they are nothing like their ancestors, we often exhibit similar inclinations. Resistance to the Holy Spirit remains prevalent among many. Consequently, every believer must remain vigilant and receptive to the Lord's promptings. Missing out on the ongoing work of Jesus would be a tragedy.

The Residue of the Past

Many pray for a fresh move of God but still camp around the residue of older religious forms. That's what the Pentecostal preachers were doing when I was young. They clung to the hope that the "old bones" would bring about a miracle. Yet believers are not called to keep lying on Elisha's bones (see 2 Kings 13:20–21). It's time to set our eyes on something new.

A spiritual awakening ignited in the chapel service at Asbury University in Wilmore, Kentucky, on February 8, 2023, prompting hundreds of college students to seek the face of the Lord. Testimonies of transformation swiftly circulated, captivating the hearts of many.

Amid this rising hunger, a seasoned ministry leader visited the services. However, he failed to grasp the significance of what was happening. Critically, he remarked, "If this truly is a revival, it isn't much of one. They need to recruit some decent worship leaders— people who can sing the songs in tune. Haven't they ever heard of excellence? Also, it wouldn't hurt for them to enlist some better preachers. A genuine revival isn't some kind of amateur hour."

Because he had a preexisting matrix for revival, this leader couldn't comprehend what was going on in Kentucky. It seems that he dismissed what he didn't understand.

Madison Pierce, a student at Asbury Theological Seminary at the time, offered a differing perspective. He shared, "I come from a spiritual background that has left me weary of hype in a culture of spectacle. I've grown tired of disintegrous representations of divine work. . . ."[1] He was struck, however, by what he was witnessing at Asbury. Here, he wrote that he was encountering these:

A tangible sense of peace for a generation with unprecedented anxiety

A restorative sense of belonging for a generation amidst an epidemic of loneliness

An authentic hope for a generation marked by depression

A leadership emphasizing protective humility in relationship with power for a generation deeply hurt by the abuse of religious power

A focus on participatory adoration for an age of digital distraction[2]

Pierce reiterates, "It feels as if God is personally meeting young adults in ways meaningful to them. My generation was formed differently. . . ."[3] Drawing on these distinctions, he writes that the meetings were marked "by a tangible feeling of holistic peace, a restorative sense of belonging, a non-anxious presence through felt safety, repentance driven by experienced kindness, humble stewardship of power, and holiness through treasuring adoration."[4]

This young man commented, "I don't want to make the mistake of trying to fit this new work into old paradigms. The new wine cannot be understood with the old expectations of revival."[5] That seems a fair admonition for any believers who harbor preexisting ideas about revival. While moves of God often share common elements, no two are identical. Each generation has its own idiosyncrasies and needs.

Sadly, some established believers harbor animosity toward newer moves of God. They find fault with trifling matters and are unwilling to embrace anything that does not place them in the forefront. They only seem to like the parades that they're leading.

Are You Willing to Move with God?

As God moves, Christians are called to move with Him. This isn't always easy. The kind of encounters that bring believers into deeper places with God may not be what will keep them there. Entrenched methods, even if they were once fruitful, wane with time.

Older believers whom I've encountered over the years tended to lean on the methods that brought them into the Kingdom years before. But others didn't always see the relevance. Moses told the ancient Israelites that day-old manna stinks (see Exodus 16:19–29). That reality is still true.

I remember meeting a man who was prominent in the Charismatic Renewal in the 1970s. Although he understood the diverse operations of the Spirit, he was stuck in the past. He wanted to emulate Kathryn Kuhlman's ministry, but this approach felt dated. Whenever a fresh move of God was discussed, he grew angry. This entrenched leader didn't want to be argumentative, but he was bothered that the rules had changed in the middle of the game. He growled, "I already see the sick healed. I don't need anyone to explain spiritual gifts to me. I have the fullness of the anointing in my life. A lot of this other stuff is just foolishness." He didn't like the modern music or approaches to prayer. After interacting with this man, I felt as though the Lord said to me, *Learn a lesson. Don't get caught up in the past—no matter how glorious it appears. Keep moving forward.* Over the years, I have tried to stay true to this admonition.

Individuals who want to keep in step with the Spirit must keep growing. We need to be filled and then refilled. In Acts 13:52 (ISV), we observe that "the disciples continued to be full of joy and the Holy Spirit." It wasn't merely a single encounter. They experienced these fillings repeatedly. The apostle Paul reiterated, "keep on being filled with the Spirit" (Ephesians 5:18 ISV). An empowered Christian life should never be perceived as a singular occurrence. Instead, believers should continue to press in for all that the Lord has for them.

Comfort and complacency are never the goal for a Spirit-filled believer. No matter how one frames things up, change is still the price that must be paid for Kingdom advancement.

It's also important to keep this in mind: A believer who wants to see the Kingdom advance should be humble, curious, and apt to listen. Over the years, I've found inspiration in individuals who have navigated this well. One such person is the late missionary and evangelist Lester Sumrall. Beginning his ministry in classical Pentecostalism, Sumrall later openly embraced the Salvation-Healing Revival, the Charismatic Renewal, and Word of Faith ministries, as well as other movements. Sumrall was constantly pivoting and adapting in his pursuit of revival. He once said,

I want to be where the anointing is on people. I refuse to get stuck in some place or group where the Holy Spirit is not being poured out. If you are not willing to move with God, then you need to understand that God is on the move, and you are not.[6]

Sumrall carried this hunger and curiosity with him all the way to the grave. He never stopped pursuing a fresh move. What about you—are you still running after God?

Although I'd like to believe I'm receptive to anything orchestrated by God, I must admit, I probably am not. It disheartens me to know that I sometimes become as entangled in religion as anyone else. While the Lord desires a movement, I am inclined to construct a monument. John Wimber once said, "Every time we come to cross a new threshold, it costs us everything we now have. Every new step may cost us all the reputation and security we have accumulated up to that point. It costs us our life."[7]

The price to advance in the things of God will always be your entire life. When Jesus declared, "Seek first the kingdom of God," He meant it (Matthew 6:33 NKJV). Those who run after God should never let up until they catch Him.

Find Out What God Is Doing

Recognizing and aligning with what God is doing will place a demand on your life. Gideon had to grapple with this, and you probably will as well. Don't let a familiarity with tradition hinder you from discerning a fresh move of the Spirit.

Arthur Wallis, a historian and expositor, aptly conveyed this sentiment when he said, "If you would make the greatest success of your life, try to discover what God is doing in your time, and fling yourself into the accomplishment of his purpose and will."[8] By remaining open to the Spirit, you can align with God and help bring about the transformation of the world. This is accomplished by allowing God to take you "from glory to glory" (2 Corinthians

3:18 NKJV), transforming all of who you are. It's time to become a new wineskin. In essence, our challenge is not a scarcity of wine; it's a lack of suitable containers to hold it.

Keep in mind that the advancing Kingdom is not about your preferences or even your personal development. Instead, it is about the work of the Lord in the nations. Rather than trying to persuade God to bless your endeavors, take the time to look into what He is already doing in the world. Jesus once said, "My Father is always working, and so am I" (John 5:17 NLT). Whenever you see Jesus at work in something, get behind it. Don't wait. Run!

The key to all of this lies in staying receptive to the Lord. We must diligently seek to discern His activities and align ourselves with His purposes. By doing so, you can experience a profound sense of fulfillment and contribute to the flourishing of the nations.

PART 2

ENCOUNTERING

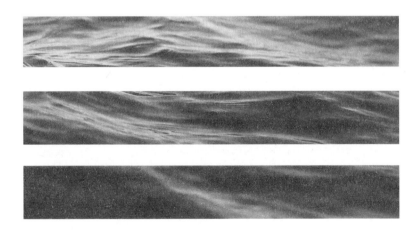

7

RESPONDING TO GOD

*What Are You Doing
with What God Has Given You?*

▌ STEVE GRAY

It was time for an extravagant offering—the only proper response to a visiting angel:

> Gideon replied, ". . . Don't go away until I come back and bring my offering to you."
> He answered, "I will stay here until you return."
> Gideon hurried home. He cooked a young goat, and with a basket of flour he baked some bread without yeast. Then, carrying the meat in a basket and the broth in a pot, he brought them out and presented them to the angel, who was under the great tree."
>
> Judges 6:17–19 NLT

When God comes near to us, we must respond. It's not enough to have faith that He is working in our lives. There is no faith without a faith response. Faith is not, as many seem to think, just a mental exercise. This was the crime—faithlessness—that Israel committed in response to the ministry of Jesus. For centuries, the Jews had promised to welcome and celebrate the coming of the Messiah. Then the Messiah arrived, the Kingdom broke in, and all their promises were suddenly forgotten. While prodigals came home and outcasts, tax collectors, and prostitutes were rescued and redeemed, religious leaders had a different response. Their hearts turned cold; their necks became stiff. Their lack of faith eventually brought judgment upon the entire nation.

Unfortunately—and I say this tenderly—many believers seem to follow that pattern in their personal lives. As with Israel, the Kingdom draws near to us, but we suddenly have little time and little heart for it. We discover it doesn't capture our interest or inspire a proper response. We proclaim Jesus is our King, but our treatment of Him when He moves in our lives shows that we are still the ones sitting on the throne. Like King Herod, we remain unimpressed by the King of the Jews. We wouldn't mind having His Kingdom, as long as we can keep the things of the world at the same time.

It's a sad situation that reminds me of the rich younger ruler. His riches got in the way of a proper response to Jesus' invitation to follow Him (see Matthew 19:16–24). Most of us don't have great riches, so we excuse ourselves. But each of us has riches and rulership of a sort—something we value that God may call us to give up. At the very least, we rule our own lives. How many of us walk away sad, unable to hand what we value over to Jesus?

As the passage from Judges 6 shows, individuals in ancient times grasped the importance of an honorable response. This is one reason Gideon stands as such a hero. As soon as he realized he was in the presence of an angel, he acted honorably, sacrificially, and worshipfully. He quit what he was doing to prepare an offering. In a time when finances and resources were impossibly strained, Gideon didn't hesitate to bring something substantial to the Lord. He went home, prepared a young goat, and made bread.

This wasn't just being a good host; it was an all-out response to the Lord, who was drawing near.

I've seen things like this occasionally in real time. One evening at the conclusion of worship time in our church, a shrill scream came from the back of the room. Suddenly, the screams turned into praise. Without warning, a woman came racing toward the front.

"I'm healed!" she shouted. "I can walk! I can walk!"

She proceeded to tell us all that she had been scheduled to have a leg amputated in just a few days. She had driven all the way from New Mexico to Kansas City, believing that if she could just step onto our church's property, she would be healed. She later testified that as soon as she did step onto the property, she started feeling the presence of God pulsate in her dead leg. When the miracle came, her response was loud and disruptive, but it spurred others to believe in faith for their healings. God honored her faith response and saved her leg.

Responding When in Trouble

The Hebrews of old knew how to respond honorably to God in their times of great need, and so should we. Like them, we need to posture ourselves to receive His creative, renewing, restoring hand of help. One of the best examples of this is laid out for us in Psalm 51, David's response to being caught in grievous sin. Like Gideon, David was a man in trouble, though of a different kind. He penned the famous words in verses 10–12 (NIV):

> Create in me a pure heart, O God, and renew a steadfast spirit within me. Do not cast me from your presence or take your Holy Spirit from me. Restore to me the joy of your salvation and grant me a willing spirit, to sustain me.

David was admitting that his heart had been impure, but if we're genuinely honest about it, most people cannot abide such a thought about themselves. Our society is so anti-condemnation that at times we won't hear the corrective voice of the Lord. He points out some area of sin or unrighteousness, and we declare it's the devil trying to put a guilt trip on us.

Is it? Or is it the sound of our hearts telling us the truth? The apostle John mentioned that our hearts can at times condemn us—and this is not the work of the enemy. Rather, it's our hearts diagnosing us and resonating with the voice of the Holy Spirit. We need to be like David and accept a correct diagnosis of our situation, or we will remain ignorant of our real problems.

Today, instead of listening to their hearts for the corrective words of the Holy Spirit, most believers reject any notion of fault and instead spend all their time trying to get more people to love and accept them as they are. Meanwhile, their hearts are telling them to change directions, to repent. How many times do we seek Christian fellowship, wanting a support group or personal cheerleading squad rather than a clear-eyed assessment of who we are and what we're doing right and wrong? If we're prone to some sin and harmful behavior—like gossip, or causing strife and division, or lying—we need to hear a corrective word that resonates with our hearts. But church life seems mostly about making people feel comfortable, when in fact a lot of people need to stay on the hot seat and hear the truth from Spirit-filled people around them until they cry out, as David did, "Create in me a pure heart!"

I love that word—*create*. It reminds us that God is greater than anything in all of creation, including our hearts and our problems. He created the heavens and the earth. He can create solutions for our troubles. Whatever the issue is, I like to use that word, *create*, to ask God to intervene.

Don't ring up a friend, go to coffee, and boohoo about other people and how they treated you. Own up to what's inside you. The world is rife with spiritual malaise, sluggishness, worldliness, selfishness, greed, and all sorts of unrighteousness. Whether we mean it to happen or not, this stuff gets in us, even as Christians, and we find ourselves stumbling when we don't realize it. Maybe you haven't been off course for very long, but something has knocked you off lately. Don't waste time searching for excuses. Go for the quick diagnosis: *God, I need your creative power. This trouble is too hard for me. It's overshadowing my heart, but you are greater than my heart. Now, God, create an escape for me from where I am, and start by purifying my heart. I'm not looking to blame anyone else.*

As David's situation shows, this creation process can be a battle and involve casualties, but God will set things right. His creative power knows no limits. It always wins.

The second verb in these Psalm 51 verses is *renew*, which is a great word because it tells us God can resurrect anything we've allowed to die. Many Christians really believed God's promises at some point in the past, knowing by faith that He could do what they asked. They served God, read the Bible, took their families to church, prayed, and much more. Yet somewhere along the line, the life ebbed out of it for them. If this happened to David, Israel's greatest earthly king, then we, too, can find ourselves in need of spiritual renewal. I'm sure David felt as you and I do sometimes— that the promises of God had slipped through his fingers, that he was disqualified because of this reason or that. But he boldly sang the fact that he wanted his walk renewed, wanted to be steadfast in God's promises again.

As with creating a pure heart, renewing is not something we can do on our own. The best we can do is accept the diagnosis that says we need to be renewed, some way, somehow—and ask God to do the work. David continued, "Do not cast me from your presence" (Psalm 51:11 NIV).

I like the way David saw things. He knew that renewal takes place in the presence of God, the same way life comes to the earth by the shining of the sun. I have noticed, and maybe you have, too, that when I feel alone or abandoned, it's often God's signal that I need to find Him again. In times like these, God waits to see if we value Him enough to draw close to Him once again. "Draw near to God and He will draw near to you," as James 4:8 (NKJV) tells us.

Have you been there? While it's true that God never leaves us nor forsakes us, there are times when we just don't sense His presence because something isn't right. God suddenly seems hard to find. David's prayer indicates the surprising fact that, in a sense, God sometimes casts people away from His presence. That's a harsh reality, but He doesn't distance Himself to condemn us. He does it to draw our attention toward Him again, to inspire us to value closeness with Him so much that we change whatever needs changing so we regain Him, so to speak. When Adam and Eve sinned, what did God do? He cast them out of the Garden. It has been His pattern throughout the Bible that for our own good, He sometimes makes Himself harder to find.

Maybe that's where you are. You're having trouble, and God seems hard to find. I assure you, He isn't pushing you away. His love is trying to pull you closer to Him. Instead of giving up on yourself, wrestle it out, run back to Him, and declare as David did, *Don't cast me from your presence. Your presence is too valuable for me to lose.*

David also requested, "Restore to me the joy of your salvation" (Psalm 51:12 NIV). Strangely, some people don't want joy. Before I met the Lord, I spent time in bars and nightclubs, and there was always some guy there (sometimes it was me) crying in his beer. Misery loves company, and inevitably other people would join the guy singing his woes. Soon, they would almost be happy about it. Those people weren't interested in being joyful. Imagine walking into that situation and saying, "How many of you would like the joy of your salvation renewed?" They would boo you out of the place. They would rather have another round of beer and a sad song.

Even Christians can get stuck in a place where sadness is easier to sustain than joy. Joy contradicts their emotions in the moment; they have a hard time believing it's real. I understand that dynamic, but David knew better. He knew he would need a few ounces of joy to get through the period of correction and renewal. Some people don't want to appear joyful during a hard season because they think they'll look weird or out of their minds. But joy is the grease that gets us through difficult situations.

The last thing David asked God to do was "grant me a willing spirit." This presents a kind of catch-22. If you don't have a willing spirit, why would you ask for one? It takes a step of faith on your part. You need a willing spirit to walk in all the things God has for you; otherwise, you won't sustain the journey.

The disciples had willing spirits but weak bodies. Jesus told them that, the night before His crucifixion. They couldn't stay awake and pray with Him in His greatest hour of need. He clarified what was happening: "The spirit is willing, but the body is weak!" (Matthew 26:41 NLT). That has been such a revelation to me. Rather than view it as a negative, we can see a lot of upsides in this statement. Jesus saw past their weak flesh to the place down deep inside, where they had willing spirits. This has encouraged me many times when I see weaknesses in myself. I think, *I do have a willing spirit, so that gives me hope.*

It also shapes how I conduct my life and ministry. I look for people with a willing spirit. Their outsides may show a lot of rough edges and scars, but I'm prepared to give someone a lot of mercy if he or she seems to have a willing spirit. It's the key to doing the work of God well over the long haul.

Have you found yourself in a place where your spirit is willing to do what God wants, but the weakness of your flesh hinders your obedience? David's prayer is for you and me. We say, *God, grant me the willingness to do what you want me to do. Help me become the worshiper, the giver, the lover, the carer of other people that you have made me to be.*

God promised in Ezekiel 36:26 (NIV), "I will give you a new heart." Why do we need new hearts? Let's see God's assessment in the same verse: "I will remove from you your heart of stone."

That's what's wrong with us. It's not that everybody else is bad and nobody cares about us, and I didn't get enough hugs when I was in second grade. My friend likes to say, tongue in cheek, that people remain hurt and ineffective through life "because your grandma left you on the potty." I've never asked him what that means or if it happened to him, but I think it means a little kid felt deserted and never got over it.

The point is, our problems are not because of past events or other people and what they did to us. Our basic problem is that our hearts turned to stone somewhere along the way. It can happen as a child, and it can happen as an adult. It can happen as a grandpa or grandma. It can happen as a dad, as a pastor, or as a pastor's wife. Our hearts harden up. It's not someone else's fault; it's ours.

But God says He will "give you a heart of flesh." He's talking about a heart that feels again, that hurts when it's appropriate to hurt and laughs when it's time to laugh. A heart that feels the feelings of others. No human can transform a heart of stone into a heart of flesh, but God can create, renew, and restore us completely. Tell Him now, from your heart, *God, I don't want a stony heart. I want a heart that feels. I want to be vulnerable. I want to hurt and laugh and cry with those around me. Mostly, I want to feel what you feel and remain sensitive to what you want me to do.*

Go Means Moving Ahead

Go doesn't always mean changing locations. The Lord made it clear to Gideon that as God's warrior, he had to stop hiding in the winepress: "The LORD turned to him and said, 'Go in the strength you have and save Israel out of Midian's hand. Am I not sending you?'" (Judges 6:14 NIV). It was time for Gideon to move forward in the divine plan.

Go is a common word in the Kingdom. We find it throughout the Bible. But when God tells someone to *Go*, people these days usually interpret it as "change locations." In my own life, that has happened once, maybe twice, when God clearly said *Go* and it meant moving geographically. But many people hear *Go* and want to launch off to some foreign land to start a ministry. Every pastor, leader, elder, or board member has heard someone say, "God is telling me to go." With confidence, the person describes how God is leading him or her into a new season somewhere else. We play it cool, knowing it won't do any good to disagree. We leave unspoken the possibility that the person's critical opinions about the way the church did worship, or a dozen other things, were not well-received. Or the possibility that he or she decided sports were more important than church for the kids.

Typically, leaders don't want to get tangled up in these all-too-familiar conversations, so we play along as though the person has indeed heard a voice from heaven, rather than that he or she is moving on to avoid dying to self and learning to love others in a local church community. When you don't want to humble yourself or become the servant of all, of course you *Go*. How can you stay? But my experience is that those who interpret *Go* wrongly will end up unwisely wandering from church to church, never achieving their potential greatness.

God often needs you to fulfill His plan right where He planted you. If you leave, God will have to raise up somebody else. God's *Go* almost always means, "Move ahead in what I have told you to do." It means obeying Him, usually right where you are. That was Gideon's type of *Go*. He was to be the man God made him to be in his own present circumstance. God called him to *Go* right where he was.

The Strength of Weakness

People have a lot of ideas about the kind of people God will use. They imagine Him calling people who have impeccable pedigrees, or a special category of brilliance, or everything lined up just right.

But God is known for using people no one else would pick—the unexpected ones, those toward the bottom of our lists.

Gideon asked the Lord, "But how can I save Israel? My clan is the weakest in Manasseh, and I am the least in my family" (Judges 6:15 NIV). One of the things that sticks out to me about Gideon's life is his evident weakness. It reminds me of the profound and well-known passage in Paul's second letter to the Corinthians, chapter 12, where Paul talks about boasting in his weakness. Personally, I'm embarrassed by weakness and usually don't want people to know if I'm feeling bad or powerless in some area of life, whether physical, spiritual, or emotional. I simply don't like talking about these areas, so most people aren't privy to what's really going on in my life.

But the revelation I've had about my weaknesses, hurts, and frailties is that they're the very things that keep me running after God. I ask God to take them away so I can feel strong, self-sufficient, and brimming with self-esteem. Every time a weakness surfaces, I seek to make it go away as quickly as possible. But that's the wrong direction. I've learned that when big trouble hits my life, it usually changes me in deep and lasting ways. As Paul made clear, weaknesses are the greatest avenue for the demonstration of God's power. Why would I want to get rid of the aspects of myself that God particularly wants to empower?

This came home to me forcefully in a series of situations, in which I couldn't get God to discipline or rebuke people who were causing me trouble. I felt let down. Why wouldn't He deal with the people who were vexing me, harassing me, treating me unfairly? I prayed and said, *I thought that's how this worked. I'm your child. I'm in the ministry. You're the dad—you go beat up people who harm me and my ministry.* If He had done that, I would have felt an immediate sense of victory—but I wouldn't be who I am today. God wants to teach us His ways, which operate by His sufficient grace, not our power.

Paul had it rougher than I did. He started a great church, and then opponents rose up to take it off course. They said Paul wasn't an apostle, that he was weak, and that he didn't speak well or have the visions others had. His opponents were full of boasting about their visions and dreams.

In my case, God had to get rid of abundant measures of conceit, anger, and revenge, and He did it in this way: Every time I asked Him to go after my opponents, He told me something like, *Here's the problem: You are so upset about the lies that people speak, but you've never been upset about the truth that I speak, that you've ignored. You've always gotten upset about the lies, but you've never been stirred about the truth. I've been speaking truth to you your whole life, and it never bothered you that you didn't pay attention. But let one person tell a lie about you, and you're ready to call down hailstones and fire on him.*

After you go through that a few times, you stop bringing your opponents before God, asking for them to be punished. Because He replies, *Are you upset about the truth yet? Are you digging it out because you're upset that Jesus is the truth and people don't care? Is it driving you? Are you preaching it? Are you teaching it? Are you praying it?*

It's a trap God sets for me so that I can't even be mad at people, because every time I get mad at them, God tells me I'm a worse liar because I know the truth and don't pay attention to it enough! I don't preach it or pursue it enough. I ignore so much truth. This process makes me feel weak and insufficient—which is exactly where God wants me. Now I'm less conceited, less inclined to defend myself against everything that makes me feel weak. I bring it to the Lord and say, *God, I feel weak tonight, but I have to get up and help people. I've got to speak to their souls and bring some truth.*

I can almost hear God say, *You're not such a hotshot anymore, huh?*

I respond, *No, I'm not a hotshot. I don't know how to preach. I don't know how to help these people.*

It sounds strange, but it's as though I can feel God asking, *Are you still going to go out there and speak for Me, though you feel so weak?*

I reply, *Yeah, God, I'm dumb enough to do it. I'm a needy vessel, like a gun with no bullets, a bow with no arrows. I'm completely empty, but I'm going to go anyway.*

That's when He says, *If you're going go out there, and you have nothing left, then your only choice is to get something from Me.*

That's where we're supposed to be. Don't be afraid to lose your self-sufficiency. Don't work your whole life to get rid of every weakness so you can finally say, *There, God, I did it. I cleaned my life up. Now I'm a better person. Now let's go minister.*

God's response would be something like, *I can't deal with a conceited person, so I'm not going to do anything with you. I can work with sinful, weak, stupid, foolish people. I've got a plan for all of that, but pride and ego can't stand before Me.*

Want to be strong in life and in strengthening others? Boast about how weak you are, because when you are weak, then you are strong. That's when the special presence of God and His anointing fall upon you. People want to be around you, and they don't even know why. It's because the favor and peace and blessing of God ride on your inabilities, weaknesses, lack of self-assuredness, and lack of self-esteem. It takes a bold person to walk into a situation empty-handed and be empowered to reach and minister to others, completely relying on God's ability. By this point in my life, not only do I not have anything to offer, but I've stopped asking God to save my bacon so I do have something to offer. Just as the three young Hebrew men said in the fiery furnace, "If God doesn't rescue us, we're still not bowing to you. We've already made up our minds. We'd like God to spare us, but if He doesn't, it doesn't change our decision" (my paraphrase; see Daniel 3:16–18).

Instead of spending your life trying to see how big you can get, see how small you can get. The smaller you get, the bigger God will get. Don't be self-sufficient; be God-sufficient. Start that journey now. Don't wait for weaknesses or hurts to be taken away. Let Him walk the highway of your insufficiency. Gather up all your stuff and tell Him, *Here's everything I am—good and bad, scary, fun and crazy. Can we start the journey now? I feel small and ignorant, weak, and incredibly imperfect.*

God's response to you is His response to Gideon: *You're hired. You're perfect for the job.*

Uproot, Tear Down, and Destroy

Amid fighting battles over his identity in God, Gideon quickly found himself in an even more deadly battle—the one over his father's religion. To advance further in God's purposes, he was going to have to tear down his family's ancient altar of idol worship:

> That same night the LORD said to him, "Take the second bull from your father's herd, the one seven years old. Tear down your father's altar to Baal and cut down the Asherah pole beside it. Then build a proper kind of altar to the LORD your God on the top of this height. Using the wood of the Asherah pole that you cut down, offer the second bull as a burnt offering."
>
> So Gideon took ten of his servants and did as the LORD told him. But because he was afraid of his family and the townspeople, he did it at night rather than in the daytime.
>
> Judges 6:25–27 NIV

Gideon's father had built an altar to the false god Baal on a high hill. Alongside it, he built an Asherah pole. God told Gideon to tear down his father's altar to Baal and cut down the Asherah pole. Gideon—still perhaps not seeing himself as the mighty warrior God knew him to be—went at night to avoid detection. He and ten servants demolished his father's altar and built a proper altar to the Lord. There he sacrificed a second bull from his father's herd, using the wood from the detestable pole as firewood.

The next morning, the townspeople were furious and demanded that Gideon be killed. Joash, his father, stepped in and reasoned with them, saying, "If Baal really is a god, he can defend himself"

(Judges 6:31 NIV). His father's wisdom won the day, and Gideon's life was spared.

Like many of us, Gideon lived with his family's traditional religion hanging over him. Some people never fulfill God's destiny for their lives because what God asks them to do is not in line with the way they were raised. Gideon grew up around idol worship. That was the religion of his family, but he couldn't become a warrior for Israel while heeding his father's religion. Gideon had to gather the strength he had and tear down his father's altar, breaking the demonic powers of Baal.

Is it possible you're in the same battle? Is "old-time religion" or the belief system of your father and mother holding you back while God wants to do a new thing in you?

Jeremiah faced a similar challenge of traditional religion in his day. Like Gideon, he was called as a young man to fight great battles, and he argued with God about being too young to obey His command. God responded, "See, today I appoint you over nations and kingdoms to uproot and tear down, to destroy and overthrow, to build and to plant" (Jeremiah 1:10 NIV).

Again, God chose someone unqualified and weak by worldly standards. Nearly all believers want to partner with God to build and plant. What matters is how we respond. Do we respond with honor and sacrifice when God draws near? Do we allow Him to create, renew, and restore a pure heart and a willing spirit within us? Do we say yes, in spite of our frailties, and allow Him to express perfect power in our weaknesses? Do we tear down the idols of past religion?

These are not easy things to do in a culture driven today by the all-encompassing demand for love and acceptance. But only by honoring and repenting, by tearing down and sacrificing, do we clear the way for God's miraculous power to work as it did for Gideon, so God can build and plant and show Himself victorious far more powerfully than we ever could on our own.

8

FLEECES AND SUPERNATURAL LEADINGS

What's God Showing You?

| J. D. KING

Once, during an outreach in another city, I encountered a man with a cane. I had what I felt was a prompting from God to pray for him. As I approached, however, he expressed his skepticism, saying, "You're welcome to give it a try, but I don't have much faith in it."

With unwavering determination, I began to intercede on his behalf. Afterward, I asked how he was feeling. He replied, "About the same."

I was taken aback by the lack of change and started to question whether I had misinterpreted the prompting. In a quiet moment of reflection, I prayed, *Lord, I thought you led me to this man. What happened?*

Later, I encountered more resistance. A woman declined my offer to pray for her, stating, "With the way you interacted with that man, I think you might be a false prophet."

This was so disheartening to hear. I was trying to follow the Lord's guidance, but it felt as though I was coming up short. With a heavy heart, I left town feeling disappointed and unsure of myself.

A few days later, however, a surprising turn of events occurred. The man with the cane showed up at a Wednesday church service dressed in oil-stained overalls. No one initially paid attention to his clothes, but later in the meeting, he shared his testimony. He revealed that he had changed the oil in his daughter's car, something he couldn't do before. He said this was due to Jesus' healing power. This man's shocking testimony unleashed something powerful in that church, and the entire congregation began to seek the Lord more earnestly.

I had tried to respond to the Lord's leading, and it looked as if I had gotten it wrong. In fact, I had looked like a fool for a few days in the eyes of many. Yet Jesus knew what He was doing, and He set the right things in motion. A heavenly breakthrough ensued that changed everything.

Christians should remain open to signs from the Lord. If we listen attentively, God will help us discern where we should go. In the lead-up to a move of God, there will be leadings that help believers keep in step with the Spirit.

Laying Out a Fleece

Coming out of the winepress, Gideon was on the verge of a new beginning. But he was far from understanding what to do next. He wanted further guidance and direction. In moments like this, illumination from the Lord is priceless. Even the most devout and biblically knowledgeable Christians still need a gentle nudge from time to time. You don't know everything all on your own.

Gideon, seeking confirmation of his divine calling, placed a fleece, a piece of wool, on the ground. He asked the Lord to cause the dew to descend solely upon the wool, while leaving the soil dry. Miraculously, God granted his request. Then Gideon sought further confirmation, asking for a reversal of conditions: a dry fleece and wet earth. Once again, the Lord graciously honored his request (see Judges 6:36–40). These extraordinary signs affirmed that the Lord was, without a doubt, calling Gideon to the battle lines.

This exceptional story from the book of Judges underscores God's willingness to provide guidance to those who earnestly seek it. It also demonstrates the importance of attentiveness to the signs the Lord places before us. Sometimes these signs can show a man or woman the pathway to his or her destiny.

Many are in a tight place, trying to figure out their next steps. Maybe they would get better direction if they truly laid things out before the Lord, like Gideon. Whenever I do this, the Lord responds and gives me fresh insight into what I need to do. I believe He will do the same for you.

As Gideon laid out a fleece, his understanding of his mission grew significantly. The signs acted as a catalyst, propelling him into his God-ordained role. It's hard to step into your destiny if you aren't open to the leadings of the Lord.

Are your eyes open to the ways of God? Will you submit your life to Him and learn how to walk in the ways of grace?

Responding to the Lord's Leadings

There's a rich tapestry of Scripture that showcases God empowering people and aligning them with His Kingdom. In the New Testament, Jesus Christ embarked on a mission to reconnect humanity with the Father through the Spirit. Long beforehand, the prophet Jeremiah declared the Lord's intention to bring this forth in the life of believers. God promised to place His "instructions deep within them," inscribing these truths "on their hearts" (Jeremiah 31:33 NLT). What was once recorded on tablets of stone and parchment was now being brought to bear in the lives of believers.

The New Testament emphasizes the importance of receiving from the Lord. In the gospel of John, Jesus asserted, "If you love me, you will do as I command" (John 14:15 CEV). This principle extends beyond just an engagement with biblical texts or sound doctrine. Obviously, both are vital, but here the Lord wants His people to get in sync with His thoughts and passions. Responding to His leadings is, in fact, an act of love. Those who not only acknowledge the Lord's teachings, but also act on them are the ones who truly value Jesus.

This goes without saying, but believers need to be receptive to the Lord's promptings. You and I are being called to lean in and let the Lord guide us—even when we can't see all the next steps. The wisest man in the world, Solomon, spoke about this centuries ago: "Trust in the LORD with all your heart and lean not on your own understanding; in all your ways submit to him, and he will make your paths straight" (Proverbs 3:5–6 NIV).

Although he possessed immense wisdom, Solomon recognized the limitations of his own reasonings. He understood that submission to the Lord wasn't merely an intellectual exercise, but a point of heartfelt action.

Moving forward with signs and spiritual leadings is not without challenges—particularly if an individual is still wrestling with his or her identity and calling. That's why believers need wisdom and discernment. It's vital to build our lives on God—the one "who does not change like shifting shadows" (James 1:17 NIV).

Going Off the Beaten Path

Once, while on a road trip in Iowa, I found myself cruising along I-35. My radio was blasting worship music, and I was absorbed in intercessory prayer. Oblivious to the specifics of my route, I was relying solely on the guidance of the GPS.

Suddenly, I felt a subtle nudge. It was as if the Lord whispered, *Change your course.* I wasn't sure what to think, but I decided to heed this prompting, so I pulled off into a gas station nearby.

There, amid the pumps and convenience store snacks, I took a moment to reevaluate my journey. I discovered that a quaint country road could take me to the same destination. With time on my side, I took the detour, excited by the prospect of encountering a few more charming barns along the way.

Veering off I-35 turned out to be providential. Later, I heard news of a horrific accident along the very section of highway I had chosen to avoid. A multiple-car pileup had caused injuries and brought traffic to a standstill. If I had remained on my original route, I could have been injured or trapped in a traffic jam. I felt as though the Lord was looking out for me, and I'm so thankful I responded to His gentle nudge. I always try to pay attention to the Lord's leadings. He will help us find the right way to go.

Led in a Roundabout Way

I know a lot of people who have a constrained worldview. They only believe what they encounter through their five senses. They would never be open to the supernatural leadings that come from the Lord. They don't realize that their beloved earthly wisdom pales in comparison to that which is spiritual.

The apostle Paul says, "The natural person does not accept the things of the Spirit of God, for they are folly to him, and he is not able to understand them because they are spiritually discerned" (1 Corinthians 2:14 ESV). This verse highlights the disparity between earthly wisdom and spiritual illumination. True wisdom encompasses a deeper understanding that transcends the natural sphere.

Scripture gives us examples of many people receiving leadings from the Lord. One of the most compelling comes from Acts 16. Paul and Silas had their sights set on a journey to Asia. As they encountered unexpected challenges, however, they found themselves detained in Phrygia and Galatia. Undeterred, they redirected their course northward toward Bithynia, only to have to go in yet another direction. Instead of yielding to discouragement or frustration, these men pressed on, charting a path through Mysia that eventually led them to the port of Troas. Paul finally experienced a heavenly vision that made everything clear. The apostles' assignment was now in Macedonia:

> That night Paul had a vision: A man from Macedonia in northern Greece was standing there, pleading with him, "Come over to Macedonia and help us!" So we decided to leave for Macedonia at once, having concluded that God was calling us to preach the Good News there.
>
> Acts 16:9–10 NLT

This story underscores the importance of placing our trust in the Lord's guidance, even when our journey diverges from our initial plans. Signs, when interpreted correctly, serve as valuable tools that allow us to grasp God's will. It's crucial to continue progressing, even when the ultimate destination remains obscured.

Sometimes the road may be arduous, moving slowly across difficult terrain. Believers need to trust the Lord as they move. After the Israelites were released from Pharaoh's grip in Egypt, strikingly God "did not lead them along the main road that runs through Philistine territory, even though that was the shortest route," because He was concerned that if they were "faced with a battle, they might change their minds and return to Egypt" (Exodus 13:17 NLT). Therefore, the Lord "led them in a roundabout way" (verse 18).

God perceives events from every perspective, possessing a profound awareness of what's unfolding beneath the surface. He knows that many times, the longer route is the best path for us to take. You and I may not like that fact, but we need to continue trusting in His wisdom and leadings.

Although centuries have passed, the Lord still speaks. Are you listening?

Demanding Signs

When God draws near, remarkable signs often occur. The Lord graciously shows the way forward, particularly during seasons of uncertainty. God captures the attention of His sons and daughters, encouraging them to move in new directions.

Sadly, some Spirit-filled believers are too caught up in the spectacular. They get entangled in an entertainment mindset, yearning for bizarre displays and sideshow antics. I know many who search for this in online videos. Although the Lord regularly engages our imagination, it isn't helpful to fixate on sensational things. The Kingdom of God isn't frivolous.

Jesus once addressed Galilean crowds, saying, "You came looking for me because I fed you by a miracle, not because you believe in me" (John 6:26–27 TPT). Some followers bounced around city to city, enjoying the free food and miracles, but they weren't interested in discipleship. Some pressed Him for stupendous displays—ignoring the fact that He had already provided plenty to see. When this happened, the Son of Man rebuked them, saying, "Only an evil, adulterous generation would demand a miraculous sign" (Matthew 16:4 NLT).

Jesus healed the sick, cast out demons, and fed the hungry, but some demanded even more dramatic displays. Even to this day, some Christians fail to recognize that they're being pulled in the wrong direction with their insistence on being entertained.

In the mid-twentieth century, during the Salvation Healing (1947–1958) and Latter Rain (1952–1965) revivals, the crowds lost their sense of awe. Instead of being satisfied with simple acts of grace, many demanded novel teachings and sensationalistic displays. This was one of the primary reasons why these moves of God ended prematurely.

I notice a similar superficiality among modern Pentecostals and charismatics. Some are overly focused on extraordinary signs, missing other components the Lord is revealing. This is unfortunate. It's time to see who Jesus is and what He has already accomplished.

Real faith senses when a matter is closed. So when a clear path from the Lord is apparent, additional confirmations are unnecessary. I'm grateful for God's patience as we process His leadings, but it's crucial for each of us to undergo personal growth. We must take responsibility and keep advancing. When you finally know what the Lord wants, don't argue. Obey.

The Sign Is Not the Revival

In Scripture, signs served as aids that facilitated people's recognition of Jesus. Signs helped them become aligned with the order of God's Kingdom. Rather than being the mission itself, signs and wonders function as signposts, directing the focus of God's people toward a deeper spiritual reality.

To illustrate this concept, let's consider the analogy of a restaurant sign. While a lit-up billboard may attract the attention of passersby, it's the food that satisfies hunger, not the sign. No one stops in to eat wires, paint, and metal. Similarly, signs and wonders that are present in and around the Church should not be the believer's primary concern. Instead, these displays effectively redirect our attention to the greater reality of Christ and His Kingdom.

Some of the older intercessors understood this truth. Charles Grandison Finney, for example, said,

The apostles employed miracles, simply as a means by which they arrested attention to their message, and established its Divine authority. But the miracle was not the revival. The miracle was one thing; the revival that followed it was quite another thing. The revivals in the apostles' days were connected with miracles, but they were not miracles.[1]

Sadly, some Spirit-filled believers become so caught up in pursuing supernatural signs that they miss other things the Lord is revealing. Aligning with God's purposes does not always necessitate seeing angels or any other extraordinary spectacle. Often, a simple word from Scripture is sufficient. Don't be distracted by frivolous things and miss what matters.

It's important to remain attentive to the guidance of the Lord, but also to place it in the proper context. Ask the Lord for help as you advance.

Openness

Gideon's life was profoundly impacted as he received divine guidance. For him, it came by a visitation. The Lord awakened his calling during a crucial period in Israel's history. Through marvelous encounters, he was guided in the right trajectory. In moments of uncertainty, God provided unmistakable clarity. It's important to understand that believers are not meant to be kept in the shadows.

Gideon saw and felt the message of God, but the Lord can direct us in several different ways. For you, God's guidance may come by other means. Be open to all He is saying.

Those who yearn for a deeper work of the Lord should remain receptive to the Spirit's promptings. Signs will arise that can redirect our attention to Jesus. Even in the present day, God remains in constant communication with His children. The pivotal question we must ask ourselves is, Are we attuned to His voice?

9

A SOUND
FROM HEAVEN

How Clearly Can You Hear?

J. D. KING

As God moves on the earth, He unleashes a sound. It is a thundering resonance that gathers and empowers believers—positioning them to advance with the glories of the Kingdom.

I can attest to the incredible things that happen when the Lord draws near. During holy moments, I have heard frequencies that defy explanation. These sounds affected me at the deepest levels of my being. It's an experience that fills me with awe and wonder.

Once, during a Friday evening worship service, hundreds of voices soared to the heavens in a way that left me trembling. It's difficult to articulate the magnitude of what occurred, but inexplicable sounds filled the room.

As the atmosphere filled with the Lord's presence, the wavelengths increased. I heard sounds that were beyond human expression—notes of higher highs and deeper lows than I had ever heard. In that moment, it felt as though the beauty of earthly praise was melding with the glories of heaven.

It may sound surreal, but as we sang, we felt as though we were joining the angelic hosts in their worship of the Almighty. There's nothing quite like hearing voices of flesh and blood harmonize with the heavenly choir.

This auditory phenomenon is not unique. It has been reported in other revivals such as the Second Awakening (1801–1830), the Welsh Revival (1904–1905), the Pentecostal Revival (1906–1913), and the Latter Rain Revival (1952–1965).

Frank Bartleman, a Baptist intercessor, had an encounter like this while he attended the Azusa Street Revival in Los Angeles, California (1906–1909; this was the beginning of the Pentecostal Revival). He described it as follows:

> The spirit of song given from God in the beginning was like the Aeolian harp in its spontaneity and sweetness. In fact, it was the very breath of God, playing on human heart strings, or human vocal cords. The notes were wonderful in sweetness, volume, and duration. In fact, they were ofttimes humanly impossible. It was "singing in the Spirit."[1]

Others shared similar stories. A. W. Otto attended Maria Woodworth-Etter's convention in Connecticut in the summer of 1913 and documented some remarkable things. Describing the sound he heard, Otto proclaimed,

> It began on the right side of the audience, and rolled from there over the entire company of baptized saints in a volume of sounds resembling in its rising and falling, its rolling and sinking, its swelling and receding character, the rolling waves of the ocean when being acted upon by the wonderful force which produces the tides.[2]

What I heard in the Friday evening service is still etched in my memory. Ethereal sounds filled the room, moving in multiple dimensions—gripping all my senses. I heard a thousand tiny cymbals crash, and bass swells that sounded like the depths of the ocean.

I couldn't take it all in, or even grasp all that was transpiring, but I knew God was in it. The Bible verse about God inhabiting the praises of His people made sense to me for, perhaps, the first time (see Psalm 22:3 NKJV). In these harmonious moments, heaven and earth intermingled, and I felt a connection to something much bigger than myself.

Inexplicable sounds were calling me to arise and respond. The men and women who had gathered couldn't sit back; we had to press into all that the Lord had for us.

The things we believers hear are calling us to a higher place.

A Sound Is a Call to Arms

In God's Kingdom, the Spirit, sound, and activation intersect. This is exemplified in Gideon's story in the Old Testament. As God spoke to this wheat thresher, one of Gideon's first actions was to notify his fellow warriors of the upcoming battle. The Bible records, "Then the Spirit of the LORD clothed Gideon with power. He blew a ram's horn as a call to arms, and the men of the clan of Abiezer came to him" (Judges 6:34 NLT).

The glory of God rested on Gideon and empowered him to accomplish a glorious mission. As the Spirit descended, he emitted a loud sound. Gideon's shofar blast reverberated through the hearts of the tribesmen, and they paid heed to this holy summons. With the emergence of a sound, a new era had begun, and nothing would remain the same.

The sounding of the shofar was first instituted on Mount Sinai during the time of Moses (see Exodus 19:13). In addition to signaling and activating, the long blast of the ram's horn reasserted

God's power.[3] Complex realities were in play as the shofar sounded. Michael Strassfeld writes,

> There is a sense of expectation in the silence before the shofar sound, followed by unease evoked by the various blasts. Part of its mystery lies in the interplay of the silence, the piercing sound, and the hum of the people praying. On its most basic level, the shofar can be seen to express what we cannot find the right words to say. The blasts are the wordless cries of the People of Israel. The shofar is the instrument that sends those cries of pain and sorrow and longing hurtling across the vast distance towards the other.[4]

Later, in the book of Judges, Gideon gathered a small company of men armed with nothing but rams' horns. To the casual observer, it would seem like a futile plan to have three hundred farmers making a long blast against the Midianites (see Judges 7:16–22). Yet this unconventional strategy worked. God utilized a sound burst to enact a victory.

The weaponization of sound wasn't common in ancient warfare. Armies used swords, spears, and slings—not rams' horns. The Lord, however, isn't concerned with human strategies. He often colors outside the lines.

Just as thunder can shake the earth and announce the arrival of a storm, the sound of the rams' horns in Gideon's time signaled the incursion of God's Kingdom. These sounds caused things to rattle and shake. When the earth reverberates with heavenly glory, the people of God need to make their move.

A Mother's Cry and Clanging Swords

Sounds can unlock powerful realities. There have been instances when the reverberations go much farther than any of us can imagine. I recall a group of students who, during lunch breaks at Lee's Summit Academy, a private Christian K-12 school in our state, cried out to God. Their earnest prayers echoed through the halls, sparking curiosity and questions. Remarkably, at least one class-mate came to Jesus as a result of their cries. People change when they hear a heavenly sound.

I also remember a young couple who wanted to borrow a refer-ence book from me. As I visited their home to deliver the hardback, a piercing shriek emanated from the living room. Several ladies had gathered to pray that night, and one of their fierce cries cut through the room. The raw emotion in this woman's voice struck everyone and unleashed the spirit of intercession. Many were deeply touched as they heard this sound.

Sometimes, soul-shaking sounds defy convention. A few years ago, I embarked on a mission trip to Argentina, where I had the privilege of speaking to some students in Resistencia. During an afternoon session, I discussed the importance of responding to the Spirit's promptings. I emphasized that believers cannot afford to remain passive when God is making a sound.

As the meeting ended, I stood to the side with my back to the crowd. As the worship team played, I interceded and waited on the Lord. I had no idea what was about to unfold, but I sensed that Jesus was about to reverberate through the room.

Suddenly, a jarring sound pierced the air. It was reminiscent of clashing medieval swords. The metallic reverberations signaled to me that spiritual warfare was underway, and that God was reclaiming His sons and daughters.

In a split second, I turned around to witness a sight that took my breath away—a hundred teenagers charging toward me. As I extended my hands in prayer, the presence of God descended on the room. Dozens collapsed to the ground as if they had been struck by lightning.

The reverberation of the Kingdom had cut through the air and demanded a response. These believing kids refused to sit back while God was making a sound. They heard, and they began to move.

Have you ever heard the clanging of swords in the Spirit? When I heard it in Resistencia, it changed everything I understood about the unseen realm. The sounds of the Kingdom not only breach barriers, but they also help us align with God. What are you hearing?

The Rolling of Loud Thunder

I was having coffee with an evangelical friend, and he asked me why Pentecostal and charismatic churches were so loud. He said, "J. D., I don't know why you worship and pray with the volume all the way up. God isn't deaf."

I laughed at his remarks and acknowledged, "I know that the Lord can hear just fine. But sometimes, believers can't!"

The Lord knows that Christians get myopic and distracted. Sometimes Jesus roars to invigorate our senses and reclaim His supremacy. It may not fit our American sensibilities, but the Kingdom of God is loud.

Throughout Scripture, we find thunderous voices and resonant frequencies. For instance, when Moses encountered God on the holy mountain, "thunder roared" (Exodus 19:16 NLT). Later, when Isaiah saw six-winged seraphim, he acknowledged, "Their voices shook the Temple to its foundations" (Isaiah 6:4 NLT). Ezekiel had a similar experience when he encountered heavenly beings. He said, "As they flew, their wings sounded to me like waves crashing against the shore or like the voice of the Almighty or like the shouting of a mighty army" (Ezekiel 1:24 NLT).

In the New Testament, John the Revelator encountered a comparable soundscape as he received a vision from the Lord. He wrote, "I heard a sound from heaven like the roar of mighty ocean waves or the rolling of loud thunder. It was like the sound of many harpists playing together" (Revelation 14:2 NLT). When men and women encounter these sounds, it shakes them out of a stupor and makes them change direction. With the reverberations of the Kingdom, all things are becoming new (see Revelation 21:5).

Like the Roaring of Niagara Falls

I told my friend that down through history, many of the moves of God were noisy. One might, for example, hear a mixture of murmurs, groans, and screams intermingled with exhortations, testimonies, and praises. This sound tapestry is dense and vast. Spiritual awakenings produce a deep resonance that reverberates across the land.

An enthralling account of the sounds of revival comes from James Finley, who was present at the Cane Ridge Camp Meeting in 1801. He wrote,

> The noise was like the roar of Niagara. The vast sea of human beings seemed to be agitated, as if by a storm. . . . Some of the people were singing, others praying, some crying for mercy in the most piteous accents, while others were shouting most vociferously.[5]

During the Welsh Revival in 1904–1905, a symphony of sound was unleashed. Across the countryside, the air resonated with a harmonious blend of singing, prayers, and exhortations. S. B. Shaw aptly captured the fervor that swept through the meetinghouses, writing, "The enthusiasm was unbounded. Women sang and shouted till the perspiration ran down their faces, and men jumped up one after the other to testify."[6]

I experienced this as well in the late 1990s. Some of the Smithton townspeople claimed to hear the worshipers as far as five miles away. Once, while I was standing in line at the post office, a man said, "You guys are loud. I heard you over the roar of the train as it passed through town."

I was astounded that six hundred people, in insulated walls, could roar so loudly. When heaven meets earth in a move of God, it's seldom quiet. Everything starts to reverberate.

When we hear the rumblings of God, it's time to respond. Run hard when you hear the sound from heaven.

Heavenly Reverberations

As Gideon advanced with the leadings of God, inexplicable sounds were released—disrupting the countryside. The Lord demonstrated that He could move through ground-shaking frequencies. During a holy visitation, sounds stir hearts.

In the second chapter of Acts, Luke describes a marvelous outpouring of the Holy Spirit. The people experienced extraordinary phenomena such as fire and wind. These displays confirmed that the Lord was present, as in the times of Moses and Elijah (see Exodus 19:16–20; 1 Kings 19:11–13). Nevertheless, the first sign that the intercessors encountered was "a sound from heaven" (Acts 2:2 NLT).

An outpouring of the Holy Spirit can take on many different forms, but on some level, it's the sound of heaven touching earth. The thundering reverberations were unmistakable to Gideon, the early believers in Acts, and the revivalists throughout history.

Are your ears attuned to the frequencies of heaven? Are you hearing God call you out of hiding? I am. We are.

10

REFRESHING STREAMS

Experiencing Freedom and Joy in the River

J. D. KING

I was raised in a stern religious culture in rural Arkansas. Many around me frowned on comic books, pop music, and movies. These things were viewed as distractions—satanic tools. As I grappled with my everyday life, sin seemed a foreboding reality. I encountered inklings of grace, but I found it hard to comprehend the goodness and mercy of the Lord.

Because of these religious experiences, I became a glutton for punishment. I suppose I was more drawn to the sin emphasis of the Pentecostals than the joyful expressions of later revivalists. One time I even said to some other believers, "We need a lot more crying in a move of God—not laughing."

Despite being around some powerful works of the Lord, my understanding was limited. I had Holy Spirit encounters and was a carrier of the Kingdom message, but I didn't grasp the immensity of the love of God. I still thought I had to strive to be worthy, and if I wasn't "swinging my fist," I didn't feel I was getting anywhere.

I was unable to recognize it at the time, but old religious impulses hindered the work of the Spirit in my life. Despite witnessing wonderful things, I was blinded to the beauty and the wonder. I was an "old wineskin," and as you know, Scripture warns that pouring new wine into a cracked, older vessel is a foolhardy task (see Matthew 9:14–17).

I thought that authentic spirituality came only from anguish. In my mind, God was an angry Judge—disgusted and reluctant to speak. So when I opened my mouth in worship or intercession, my failures were the first thing that came to my mind.

Regrettably, my posture before God was awful. I was always striving to get cleansed so He might speak or give me something. The interaction always seemed transactional and devoid of the joy that could come from simply delighting in Him.

Thankfully, the Lord began to transform me, showing me other facets of His nature. One time, I prayed and felt a burst of joy inside. Although it was stirring within, I didn't want to let it out. A friend who saw me said, "Your face was red, and it looked as if you were going to explode."

Overcoming my internal resistance, I finally let go, and the joy of the Lord overtook me. I began to see God in a different light. The old preacher that I had heard as a kid was right when he declared, "Some things in the Kingdom of God are better caught than taught." Not everything God does is so easily explained. Many truths are best conveyed through a Spirit-led encounter.

As I pressed into Jesus, I realized that my worth isn't dependent on attaining perfection, but on the incredible gift Christ bestowed upon me. As I reconsidered my status in the household of faith, I abandoned the transactional mindset and embraced the joy of my spiritual adoption. I can assure you that the streams of mercy breathe new life into rigid hearts. This happened to me, and it can happen to you too.

The rivers of revival cleanse and renew. They do far more than release the forgiveness of sin; they illuminate our true identities in Christ. The waters enable us to fathom the realities of the Kingdom of God and live out our calling with boldness. In the mercies of heaven, we are washed and made new.

Life in the Water

Gideon's calling was confirmed at a critical juncture in Israel's history. While the tribes had faced difficult things over the previous eras, the grip of the Midianites felt particularly oppressive. Many wondered when God would finally rescue them.

Change was needed. Sometimes, the lead-up to a breakthrough may require a different posture. The Lord wants us in the right location at the right time. In this pivotal moment, God instructed Gideon to bring his warriors "down to the spring" (Judges 7:4 NLT).

As we have discussed, rivers and springs are apt metaphors for revival. Cleansing and refreshing come from the streams. They enable the thirsty to drink and be restored. Many beautiful things take place on the edge of the water. This can also become a place of strategy and prophetic activation.

Gideon's anticipation grew as he assembled a multitude alongside the spring. He sensed that something remarkable would transpire in the waters. Springs were regarded as symbols of rejuvenation and renewal. As the warriors congregated around this life-giving source, they could draw nourishment and strength to embark on a journey.

The waters would serve as a testament, affirming that they were no longer destined to remain under the treachery of the Midianites. In the living streams a wellspring of hope flows, inspiring believers to rise above their circumstances and embrace the promise of a brighter future.

Inspiration surges as the Lord moves. In a subsequent encounter with Gideon, God imparted the following words: "If you are afraid to attack, go down to the camp. . . . Listen to what the Midianites are saying, and you will be greatly encouraged" (Judges 7:10–11 NLT). The children of God will often experience a profound uplift as they emerge from the streams of revival.

We live in a world gripped by turmoil and despair. There are a lot of things contrary to the heart of the Lord. Nevertheless, God brings hope. In His life-giving water, things are seen from a different angle. At a pivotal moment, the sons and daughters of the Most High God may begin imagining a world filled with goodness and joy. What's inside them becomes infectious, spreading across the countryside.

River of Delights

Those who stand along the water's edge get a chance to gaze upon the beauty and life-transforming glory of the Kingdom. I love the gratitude David expressed. This Israeli monarch thanked the Lord for the opportunity to drink from His "river of delights" (Psalm 36:8 NIV; see also verses 5–9). Jubilation is always found in these glorious waters.

Later, the Sons of Korah said, "There is a river whose streams make glad the city of God, the holy habitation of the Most High" (Psalm 46:4 ESV). These life-giving waters transform hearts and inspire us to walk in the Lord's ways.

In a different era, Ezekiel shared a vision of a river flowing from the Temple, carrying with it currents of heavenly glory. The prophet witnesses the progression of the water, gradually increasing in depth and power. Initially, the river is a gentle flow, only reaching ankle-deep. But it continues to rise, reaching the prophet's knees, and then his waist. Eventually, the waters become a raging stream deep enough to swim in. Ezekiel declared,

The waters of this stream will make the salty waters of the Dead Sea fresh and pure. There will be swarms of living things wherever the water of this river flows. . . . Fruit trees of all kinds will grow along both sides of the river. The leaves of these trees will never turn brown and fall, and there will always be fruit on their branches. There will be a new crop every month, for they are watered by the river flowing from the Temple. The fruit will be for food and the leaves for healing.

Ezekiel 47:8–9, 12 NLT

Witnessing the life-giving water emanating from the Temple, Ezekiel was awestruck. God's glorious streams overwhelm death and decay, and help usher in a renewal of creation. In this revelatory encounter, God assures Ezekiel that "where the river flows everything will live" (Ezekiel 47:9 NIV).

The imagery of a life-giving river flowing from the throne room is echoed in the New Testament. In Revelation, John witnessed a similar kind of river. He wrote,

The angel showed me the river of the water of life, as clear as crystal, flowing from the throne of God and of the Lamb down the middle of the great street of the city. On each side of the river stood the tree of life, bearing twelve crops of fruit, yielding its fruit every month. And the leaves of the tree are for the healing of the nations.

Revelation 22:1–2 NIV

This river not only satisfies; it also rejuvenates. Now more than ever, believers need an opportunity to encounter the Lord's goodness and glory. It's in the joyous waters of revival where people's hearts truly come alive.

Waves of Liquid Love

Over the years, revivals have been characterized as mass gatherings where waywardness and sin are addressed. Older preachers highlighted repentance, consecration, and self-denial. These matters are still vital. The weightier matters of the Kingdom should never be minimized. But with that said, moves of God are not always a somber affair. In fact, many have been marked by the atmosphere of laughter and joy.

John Wesley, the celebrated revivalist, described the manifestation of glory that transpired around 3:00 a.m. in one small prayer meeting. He said, "The power of God came mightily upon us, so that many cried out for exceeding joy."[1] Notably, these and other encounters played a pivotal role in carrying the Gospel into courtyards and alleyways across England.

During the Great Awakening in New England, Jonathan Edwards recorded the reactions of members of his congregation. He observed that some were on the verge of giggling: "Their joyful surprise has caused their hearts as it were to leap, so that they have been ready to break forth into laughter."[2]

Nearly eighty years later, Charles Finney recounted a profound experience he had with the Lord in the woods. He said he was inundated with "waves of liquid love."[3] God will move in the private moments of people's lives as regularly as in public gatherings.

Apparently, this was not an isolated incident for Finney. In Antwerp, New York, while he was praying, the presence of the Lord was so intense that Finney fell "spasmodic" on the floor. He wrote,

> My heart was so overflowing with joy at such a scene that I could hardly contain myself. A little way from where I stood was an open fireplace. I recollect very well that my joy was so great, that I could not help laughing in a most spasmodic manner. I knelt down and stuck my head into that fireplace, and hung my pocket handkerchief over my head, lest they should see me laugh; for I was aware that they would not understand that it was irrepressible, holy joy that made me laugh.[4]

Joy was also prominent in many of the later moves of God. Historian Vinson Synan said that overwhelming encounters of joy had a long-standing Pentecostal tradition and often served as "a kind of emotional release."[5] (I think this was particularly the case for marginalized families since many early Pentecostals were poor. My family was.) Several people have shared testimonies about this kind of release with me over the years. I remember when an elderly evangelist told me how much joy he found in the households of the believers. He said, "The saints were always bubblin' up."

When God begins to move in people's lives, it doesn't always look like what others imagine. In these seasons, individuals often get a renewed sense of hope and their mouths are filled with laughter. Outpourings are often characterized by the liberating work of Jesus. The Holy Spirit wants to bring the same joy and freedom to us today.

Joy Unspeakable and Full of Glory

Initially, I found it hard to reconcile a soul-stirring revival with expressions of infectious joy. How do these things go together? From my point of view, Christians needed to stay far away from all frivolous behavior.

Nevertheless, people who dismiss jubilant displays seem to be ignorant of how joyful God is. I remember the first time I read that the Lord "will rejoice over you with joy, He will be quiet in His love, He will rejoice over you with shouts of joy" (Zephaniah 3:17 NASB). Admittedly, that was not how I imagined God responding to people, but the truth of Scripture is unmistakable.

At the time, I discounted the idea of infectious joy because I thought it was not in the scope of the larger mission of God. I didn't realize just how much I had missed from the pages of Scripture. I somehow had overlooked the fact that joy aligns with the Spirit's power and the advancement of God's Kingdom. I somehow had overlooked that it was a sign of the emerging New Covenant age.

I'm not the only one who has thought like this. I've met many with the same misguided outlook. What does it reveal about our hearts when so many Christians discredit the value of joy? Too many are somber in their times of devotion, or when they read their Bibles. We serve the Life-Giver, so we should live.

At one point in the New Testament, Jesus took His disciples aside and said, "These things I have spoken to you, that my joy may be in you, and that your joy may be full" (John 15:11 ESV). In other words, Spirit-filled believers aren't promised a measly portion, but the fullest measure of joy.

In his first epistle, Peter talks about how those who sincerely love Jesus will encounter "joy unspeakable and full of glory" (1 Peter 1:8 KJV). I never associated a sense of jubilation with glory, but this is exactly what the apostle is describing.

In Romans, Paul points out how the Lord fills people "with all joy and peace" so they "may overflow with hope by the power of the Holy Spirit" (Romans 15:13 NIV). The apostle is talking about experiencing not just some, but all joy. This type of encounter is apparently a vital part of the Holy Spirit's work.

In Galatians 5:22, Paul highlights joy as a fruit of the Holy Spirit. As a result, we can reasonably expect it to be evident in the lives of believers. Regardless of everything else going on, the oil of gladness should be evident wherever believers go—workplaces, restaurants, churches, and everywhere else. If joy is absent, something is clearly wrong.

Although there are times to be sober-minded and earnest, gloominess and despair shouldn't continually characterize a Spirit-filled believer. If we are genuinely filled with glory, a smile ought to cross our faces every now and then.

Over and over, the Lord graciously seeps into our culture, changing hearts through His joyful displays. We can feel the life of God when we get ready to go to work or tuck our children in bed at night. Joy can erupt in every sphere.

Although it may sound strange, I can assure you that this is how the Kingdom operates. The apostle Paul said that "the Kingdom of God is . . . joy in the Holy Spirit" (Romans 14:17 NLT). It's time to recognize that the triumph of God is rooted in this inexplicable reality.

Uncomplicated

As I moved deeper into the things of God, I loved the freedom being released in my life. Nevertheless, I overlooked some expressions of the Spirit. As believers, we tend to let what we know and understand consume everything else. Some who focus on the Lord's intensity fail to grasp His tenderness. This is a problem I've had to contend with regularly.

Several years ago, Steve Gray had a remarkable encounter when he caught a glimpse of Jesus. He anticipated encountering a fierce and formidable presence, reminiscent of a warrior, but he was surprised to discover Jesus appearing "so innocent and small in stature." Gray reflected on this experience, saying, "As I gazed upon Him, I suddenly recognized how complicated I am."

Years later, this story continues to speak to me. It serves as a powerful reminder that most of us—with all of our complexities—are nothing like the meek and perfect Lamb.

God didn't call us to become so preoccupied by self-reflection. Honestly, there isn't much value in exploring all the layers of our inner worlds. Christianity in the West is so caught up in introspection. It's difficult to see anything else when you're so busy navel-gazing. I'm convinced that it's time to look upon the unencumbered simplicity of Jesus.

For years, I thought spiritually mature people were always sorrowful and stern. After becoming acquainted with world changers, however, my perspective has changed. Those who genuinely know the Lord radiate His goodness. I've observed this countless times. Joy is a poignant sign of God's presence in the life of a believer.

A Different Kind of Joy

Not everyone is open to the idea of joy. One of my evangelical friends asked me whether a move of God makes everything "sunbeams and rainbows."

I told him, "No, every believer will face awful things at some point in his or her life. The joy that emanates from heaven is not a reflection of a problem-free existence. Instead, it's the overflow of a heart graciously aligned with Jesus."

I also told him, "Some of the most joyous individuals I've encountered have found a way to rise above severe trauma." My great-uncle Eldon cared for an invalid wife for several decades in his home in rural Arkansas. He fed her, bathed her, and supplied her every need. Although the day-to-day tasks were grueling, he never stopped smiling and singing about the goodness of Jesus. He was such a wonderful inspiration.

The New Testament encourages believers to embrace joy—even amid heartache and pain. For example, Paul commended the Thessalonian believers because they "received the message with joy from the Holy Spirit in spite of the severe suffering" (1 Thessalonians 1:6 NLT). Through the Holy Spirit, people deeply rooted in the love of Jesus remain joyful—even in the face of heartache and pain.

The writer of Hebrews discusses the joy that was tied to Jesus' willingness to face the cross. He writes, "Because of the joy awaiting him," the Son of God "endured the cross, disregarding its shame" (Hebrews 12:2 NLT). In the past, I never would have associated joy with a sacrificial act. I didn't see how that could have anything to do with holiness or consecration, but it does. Laughter has the power to carry us beyond our pain and give us hope in the face of unimaginable evil.

The families I worship alongside in Kansas City war against the devil. Our voices are loud as we fight the darkness and seek the Lord. Although we've experienced remarkable victories, sometimes the enemy raises his ugly head against us. Yet even in times of disappointment, the Lord gives us "the oil of gladness instead of mourning" (Isaiah 61:3 ESV). One of the songs we like to sing declares,

> A different kind of joy,
> A different kind of joy,
> That reaches into tragedy
> And opens up my victory,
> A different kind of joy.[6]

I'm not talking about something frivolous or rooted in the foolishness of this age. I'm talking about a joy that helps you stand in the most difficult seasons.

The Kingdom of God Is Joy

Gideon and his soldiers experienced a sense of jubilation and hope as they aligned with the Lord's purposes. This ragtag army probably didn't expect to get a burst of life in such a challenging moment. People often wonder why anyone would find joy in the face of so much darkness and conflict. But people don't always understand how God operates.

Throughout history, there are moments when God's people are forced to reevaluate their value systems and how they envision the world. As they turn toward the Lord, the Spirit draws near, unveiling more of God's nature. Suddenly the veil is torn, and we are given a glimpse of a goodness beyond our wildest imagination. The Spirit of God casts off the heaviness and gives us an incredible burst of joy in every dimension of our lives.

I always thought I knew a lot about God. So it was quite an eye-opener to discover that joy is a vital part of who the Lord is. Gladness is somehow rooted in the Lord's unchanging nature.

Holiness and joy are not entirely separate in the Kingdom of God. For me, this is such a marvelous mystery.

In an era overshadowed by corruption and malevolence, the Lord's glorious river transforms everything. We need to remember that there is joy in the Holy Spirit. He will come and help you at home, work, school, church, and wherever you go.

Centuries ago, King David said, "In Your presence is fullness of joy; at Your right hand are pleasures forevermore" (Psalm 16:11 NKJV). The living waters bring jubilation and gladness to those who will receive joy. Let that be you and me.

11

ARE YOU THIRSTY?

The Importance of Yearning for God

STEVE GRAY

"On the last and greatest day of the festival, Jesus stood and said in a loud voice, 'Let anyone who is thirsty come to me and drink'" (John 7:37 NIV).

Everyone in Israel in biblical times knew what it felt like to be painfully thirsty. Water was rare. It's easy to see why the Bible's writers used extreme thirst as a picture of what it means to seek God, as the psalmist wrote: "As the deer pants for streams of water, so my soul pants for you, my God" (Psalm 42:1 NIV). Over and over, the Bible tells us we are blessed if we have a constant, even distressing, thirst that drives us to living water.

The question for us is, Are we thirsty? Do we even know what true, all-consuming thirst feels like? Or are we satisfied with other things?

When I was in college, there was a horse ranch nearby where riders could ride free-range, without supervision. Being young guys, we often went there, climbed on the horses' backs, and rode around like cowboys, as hard and as far as we could. When we were done, we headed back to the barn. I'll never forget the time we drew close to the barn and my steed got a view, or a smell, of the water trough. Suddenly, that animal went completely out of control, overpowered by thirst. I could do nothing but hold on as it galloped toward the barn at what felt like top speed. Then it lost its footing, and we both tumbled forward, the horse landing across my legs. Having been raised on the maxim that if you fall off a horse, you get right back on, I did just that, and the horse and I returned to the barn, where it drank what seemed like gallons of water. When I awoke the next day, my legs were so bruised that I couldn't walk. It took days for me to become functionally mobile again!

My point isn't that horses are dangerous or that college students do stupid things (though both those things can be true), but that thirst is a powerful motivator. That horse detected water and bolted toward it—giving me a lifelong picture of how strong thirst drives behavior. True thirst keeps us running to the river of life as if our lives depended on it.

This keeps me asking, How thirsty am I for God?

God put the people of Israel in a place without much water on purpose. They had to seek it to find it. Then, as now, God uses thirst to guide us. For example, in Gideon's day the Israelites had abandoned and disobeyed God. So the Lord gave them into the hands of Midian for seven years—until they became thirsty for freedom, at which point they cried out to the Lord. God heard them and sent a prophet, and then an angel, and then Gideon. You see, thirst works. It causes us to consider our ways and ask, Where am I, and how did I get here?

Most of all, in God's Kingdom thirst leads us to seek living water for refreshing and revelation, and for a chance to reorient our lives.

So, how thirsty are you?

Did you know it's a Kingdom requirement to seek God as if driven by terrible thirst? Jesus described it as being like a woman who lost money and swept her house clean to find it (see Luke 15:8–10). "Seek first the kingdom of God," He commanded, and elsewhere, "Strive to enter through the narrow gate" (Matthew 6:33; Luke 13:24 NKJV). Our posture must be active and unyielding.

We see this principle at work in 2 Chronicles 15, where God was troubling the people with all kinds of distress, and in their distress, they turned to the Lord. King Asa removed the detestable idols and fully committed himself to the Lord. He then assembled the people at Jerusalem, and they entered into a covenant to seek the Lord with all their hearts and souls. Here's where it gets interesting: They all took an oath pledging that anyone who would not seek the Lord must be put to death (see verse 13). That's how important spiritual thirst became to them, once they found God's living water.

Has this principle changed today, or are we just oblivious to it? Jesus made it very clear that being spiritually thirsty and seeking God first is of primary importance. Paul insisted in numerous places that we remain fervent and zealous for God. Nowhere do the gospels teach a blasé approach toward the pursuit of God. While no one in our culture would even suggest that someone who refuses to seek the Lord be put to death—and I wouldn't suggest it either—we must admit that when we look at our world, trouble and distress are everywhere. People are dying by suicide, by their own hands. They are dying from drug use, anxiety, and all sorts of other unnatural causes. It makes us ask, Is the problem a lack of thirst? Are we in distress for a reason, and is God trying to guide us to living water?

Suppose the people of one entire city somewhere in the world believed that if they sought the Lord with all their hearts, their city would experience great peace and prosperity. Is that such an outrageous idea? Doesn't the Bible promise exactly that kind of result? But these days, the idea of seeking God to avert danger or distress doesn't enter most people's heads. Turning our hearts fully to the Lord to stop trouble, whether as churches, cities, or individuals, is not on most people's radar. So we declare to heaven by our behavior that we are not thirsty enough to seek living water. And I believe we remain in distress as a result.

Revival Is Thirst

If I'm known for anything in my life so far, it's probably as a voice for revival. But what is revival? The word means so many different things to different people. Some see it as church services where people go wild and do strange things. Others think it's when congregations experience unusual manifestations of God's presence and power. Others limit revival to that two-week period when a guest evangelist preaches a series of meetings, and everyone brings the loved ones they want to get saved.

I have a different view. I say revival is thirst. It's when a person, a home group, a church, a nation—any assemblage of people— seeks the Lord with all their hearts and souls. They "gather at the river," to use an old phrase. Have you noticed how revival is often described in river language? A revival in my own lifetime was called the river by those who experienced it. In Gideon's day, he summoned people to the river. A river is where people go when they're thirsty. Revival is people departing from the normal course of life to find water. The result of that may look loud and boisterous, or it may appear quiet and intense. The packaging of revival doesn't matter. What matters is the priority that people place on God and His Kingdom. What matters is their level of thirst.

Do we really want the living water? I'm fascinated by Jesus' discernment and understanding of people. On one occasion, He spotted a man at the Bethesda pool who had been an invalid for thirty-eight years. Jesus walked up to him and asked, "Do you want to get well?" (John 5:6 NIV).

At first glance, this question seems out of place. Who doesn't want to get well? But as I've learned, the truth is that plenty of people don't want to get well. I've counseled people in about every area of life, asking, "Do you want to get out of debt?" "Do you want to heal your marriage?" "Do you want to put an end to anxiety, fear, and stress?" The answer to all these questions should be yes, but it's usually not. Many people would rather live in distress than serve the Lord. The price is too high. They aren't willing to make the trade.

Gideon had to face this sad fact in his own nation—and in his own family. His very father was an idol worshiper. When Gideon tore down his father's altar to Baal, the townspeople gathered to kill Gideon! Here a solution had arrived in their midst, and they wanted to kill the man chosen to bring it. People grow comfortable with demons and darkness and thirst. They love the powers and temporary pleasures of sin. They don't want to get well by doing as King Asa did and turning to the Lord with all their hearts. They would rather be thirsty.

I came to a place of desperate thirst after twenty years in ministry. I was dying from thirst for God and felt I wouldn't survive spiritually, emotionally, and physically without a big drink from the waters of salvation. This wasn't the kind of condition that could be fixed by boarding a cruise ship or lying on a sandy beach somewhere. God wasn't calling me to go on sabbatical; He was calling me to seek Him in a greater way than I ever had before.

I didn't know then how much God loves to be chased. As we talked about in chapter 7, sometimes when finding God becomes difficult, it's because God wants us to pursue Him until we catch Him. "Seek the LORD while he may be found," the prophet Isaiah wrote (Isaiah 55:6 NIV). When we don't do that, we find ourselves identifying with King David, who came to a place of saying, "You, God, are my God, earnestly I seek you; I thirst for you, my whole being longs for you, in a dry and parched land where there is no water" (Psalm 63:1 NIV).

At the time of my thirst, I was trying to be the perfect everything—perfect husband, perfect dad, perfect pastor. But it all fell apart, and I fell apart. The church I led was doing great, but after a time, I was not. Watching Christians try to destroy lives, including mine, broke my heart. I knew it wasn't just them; I was somehow broken and helpless to repair myself. Like Humpty-Dumpty, I fell off the wall and couldn't put myself back together again. My life felt as if it lay in pieces.

My first thought was that God was surely finished with me. Little did I know that my distress was God-inspired. As difficult as it was, trouble had created a thirst that would lead me to the river. At the time, I had heard about a revival taking place in Florida. Not knowing what it was, but needing someplace to go, broken and hurting, I made the long, lonely drive to a place called Pensacola. There, I cried out to God all day long in a hotel room. At night I attended the services, hoping for a hint from heaven of what to do with myself.

One moment impacted me powerfully during one of the revival services. I watched a man dressed in a business suit come down the balcony stairs. He looked dazed, like a man walking away from an accident and not knowing what had hit him. He found a far corner in the auditorium and fell facedown at his own private altar. It was like watching the parable of the Pharisee and tax collector come to life. The Pharisee prayed loud and proud, but the tax collector beat his chest and cried, "God, have mercy on me, a sinner" (Luke 18:13 NIV). This man I kept my eye on groaned like someone in great pain, and it seemed to me that he must have committed some great sin to be in such agony. Then it hit me. If the man laid out on the floor was the tax collector, then who was I? Was I the Pharisee, standing, watching, glad I was not like that man? A new revelation came: *This was it. This was the way to freedom.* I needed to be like that man. Whatever he had, I needed it.

I spent the next two weeks wrestling with God, then myself, then the devil. I still didn't know if I wanted to preach, and I certainly didn't want to return home and just pick up where I had left off. I hadn't made it to the river yet, but my thirst for the living water had never been so great. When the trip was over, I drove home and pulled into my parking spot at the church. It happened to be a Sunday night, and the service had already started. I could feel the music pumping, but I felt nothing. I felt as ordinary as an old shoe and had no expectation of anything.

I opened the door of the church and walked in. I smiled, looked around, spotted Kathy, and walked toward her. I never made it to her. Without warning, I was suddenly struck with what I can only describe as a lightning bolt from heaven. There, in front of everybody, I became another person. Everything changed. My attitude, my thoughts, my singing, my preaching—it all became different. I was in the river, drinking in new life. Old things passed away. I became a new creature.

No More Passive Thirst

That night—and continuing to this day—I went from being passive in my relationship with God to being aggressive. Before that moment, I had pictured a laid-back God. Like many people, I wanted a laid-back God because such a God would leave me alone. But now, I saw that passivity wouldn't lead me to pursue and encounter God. Passive thirst wasn't going to work. I thought of Jesus after He was baptized. It says He was "led by the Spirit into the wilderness" (Matthew 4:1 NIV). The word *led* doesn't mean they held hands or linked arms and casually walked into the wilderness. It means Jesus was forcefully thrust into the desert. The picture is of someone grabbed by the scruff of the neck and moved into a new place.

That idea didn't so much appeal to me before, but having found the God for whom I thirsted, I no longer wanted anything less. Dumbed-down religion wouldn't work for me again. Thirsty people are not passive people. Someone asked me when my quiet time with God was, and I asked them back, "When is your loud time with God?"

My approach to seeking God had been transformed. I saw how deadly and sinful passivity is. For example, Eli, the priest in the book of 1 Samuel, had two sons, Hophni and Phinehas, who were wicked priests. They had no regard for God. They ministered any way they wanted to, and even slept with the women who served in the temple. Eli himself wasn't wicked like that, but he was weak and passive. He knew what his sons were doing and knew it was an abomination in God's eyes, but Eli honored his sons more than he honored the will of God. He didn't correct them, so his passivity caused all three of them to die (see 1 Samuel 2:12–36).

Passivity can seem wise when it looks like honoring our spouse, our kids, our congregation if we pastor, and even our own wants. It can keep us from desperately seeking God, because instead we're focused on maintaining the comfortable status quo around us. Passivity can look prudent, but it's often evidence of a critical lack of thirst.

Years ago, I preached a series on seeking God. After the service, a man said he still didn't understand how to seek the Lord, so the following week I did an experiment. Before the service, I taped a hundred-dollar bill under a pew. No one knew it was there except me. I preached my sermon, and at the conclusion I said I would prove to them that they knew how to seek the Lord. I let them in on my secret, that underneath a pew there was a hundred-dollar bill, and the first one to find it could keep it.

Passivity was quickly overcome. In fact, chaos broke out. People flung themselves onto the floor on their hands and knees, crawling around to try to find the money. There was even a little pushing and shoving going on. Finally, one teenage boy yelled out, "I found it!"

The lesson was learned. Everyone knows how to seek. The hundred-dollar bill proved that. Now the key was to turn that energy into seeking the Lord, who loves to be chased.

Are you in distress? Does life seem like a series of troubles? Consider the fact that you are being invited—even driven—to the river. Earnestly, diligently, with the strength that you have, chase God. If you seek Him with all your heart, you will find Him ready to lead you out of a parched land and into a land of blessings—even if you are weak in your own eyes.

Thirsting Like Gideon

Gideon did not see himself as fully capable, but one thing separated him from the others in his nation. He had a thirst for God, and his thirst gave him a regard for God. He was neither wicked nor passive. He cared for God's angel by preparing a sacrifice. He cared for God's honor, even when his own life was endangered by tearing down the altar of Baal. Gideon was blessed with a thirst for what was right. As weak as he felt, his thirst to honor God turned him into a champion.

I remember as a teenager hearing the Rolling Stones song "(I Can't Get No) Satisfaction." It didn't mean much to me then, but I understand it better now. In a world where satisfaction is offered everywhere and by everyone, dissatisfaction still rules. Even followers of Jesus are by and large unsatisfied, though they have religion coming at them from every direction. During the Christmas holidays one year, I scanned the radio for traditional holiday music. I was shocked by how many religious stations were on both the FM and AM dials. Christian music, teaching, and preaching are all around us, but so is the plague of dissatisfaction. I must conclude that dissatisfaction with religion is a sign not of rebellion, but of thirst. Godly dissatisfaction is meant to thrust us forward and make us ready for something more from God. It's what I experienced leading up to my journey to Pensacola and back. It's what drove Gideon to do great exploits at the risk of his life.

One of the most obvious signs of thirst is that substitutes don't satisfy. That cruise you enjoyed last time does nothing for you now. A cabin in snow-covered woods doesn't affect you. A new car doesn't dispel the dissatisfaction. You are thirsty for God, and nothing but His presence will satisfy.

In the gospel according to Mark, Jesus says, "Love the Lord your God with all your heart and with all your soul and with all your mind and with all your strength" (Mark 12:30 NIV). There are plenty of sermons today on loving God with our hearts, souls, and minds, meaning our will, intellect, and emotions. What I don't hear a lot about is loving God with all our strength. In my view, this is where the battle and the victory take place. No one minds people loving God with their hearts, minds, and souls. But loving God with all your strength will make other believers nervous.

Strength means all that you have. It certainly includes your arms, legs, mouth, and voice. But it also encompasses your money, your assets, your family, anything of value that you possess. All of it must go on the altar of sacrifice. This is the cure for backsliding, lukewarmness, indifference, and boredom with God. Add strength to your relationship with God, and the water of God will flow and your thirst will be quenched. To walk in the deeper things of God, you must present your entire self to Him and allow Him to flow through every part of your being.

I remember being part of a conference with several well-known leaders. We were in a huge auditorium that seated several thousand people. The place was packed. The conference speakers were all lined up across the stage, with our chairs behind us. Worship began, and as it got more intense, the crowd got more intense too. Some were clapping, swaying, jumping, shouting, even crying. Onstage, it was a completely different scene. While the crowd of people threw themselves into worshiping God, the guest speakers stood like pillars of salt, motionless, with hands folded, eyes closed, seemingly paralyzed by years of religion.

Standing among these statues, I felt the nudging of God: *Stretch yourself out before Me in the midst of the congregation.*

I decided to obey. In a suit and tie, I went to my knees, and then to the floor. I lay flat out on my face before God. I knew it was the right thing to do, but I got the feeling that it was more for the other speakers, who seemed frozen in place.

At first, I closed my eyes; then I peeked at the crowd and squinted at the others on the stage. It was as if they were afraid to look. They noticed my posture, but seemed nervous. My lying flat on the floor in front of thousands didn't seem to change the other preachers at all, but it did change me. I felt a sense of exhilaration and increased exaltation. I worshiped with spirit, soul, and body. My thirst for God was again quenched because I had given Him my strength—my all—not just my emotions, thoughts, and will. All of me went onto the fire.

People who live and worship with strength are usually criticized and considered odd or even embarrassing. It's a small price to pay to pursue God with thirst and have that thirst entirely satisfied. Because when we are thirsty, we drink differently than ever before.

How Do You Drink?

Jesus said in John 7:37 (ISV), "If anyone is thirsty, let him come to me and drink!" He placed no limit on that invitation. When we come to Him needing living water, He will never say, "I know you're still thirsty, but that's all I've got right now. You'll have to stop drinking." No, the supply is unlimited. Sometimes we need to remind ourselves as we seek God that there's no shortage of water; there's only a shortage of jars.

So how do you drink? I think Gideon's experience offers a critical insight. Historically, teachers, preachers, and even scholars have tried to use symbolism and allegory to explain why Gideon chose men who cupped their hands and drank, as opposed to those who knelt by the water's edge. You have probably heard, as I have, the explanation that those who knelt and drank were more vulnerable to the enemy, while those who drank from cupped hands remained alert and ready. That's clever, but I don't think it's the real reason.

135

The reason I think God chose the 300 men who cupped their hands to their faces is simple: It was the way Gideon drank. Gideon was going to command an army to do some unusual things, like smash jars, shout together in unison, and blow trumpets. This wasn't ordinary warfare, and it was going to require an even higher level of unity and obedience than might normally suffice. Gideon was looking for those who would follow his lead precisely and trustingly. If you think about it, it's the very same pattern Jesus gives us today: *Anyone who puts his hand to the plow and looks back is not worthy of Me* (see Luke 9:62). We must follow the pattern to achieve the results.

The manner of drinking among Gideon's soldiers wasn't what ultimately mattered. The question of the day, I believe, was, "Do you drink the way Gideon does?" Down at the river, 300 men proved themselves. The other 9,700 followed the pattern they had apparently been taught. This gives us a clear warning, and it reverberates throughout Scripture. I think of Romans 12, which admonishes us that we are no longer to follow the pattern of this world but be transformed by the renewing of our minds. To be useful soldiers, we must follow the pattern of Jesus, which may be uncomfortable, even illogical. With God, logic and familiar patterns are not the goal. Jesus offers a superior wisdom—which often looks different.

How We Drink Matters

Ten thousand thirsty men stood at the river. No big deal. These men had been drinking from rivers and streams since childhood. You kneel down, put your face in the water, and drink. Drinking isn't something we think about. We do it without thinking. The 9,700 did just that. They drank the way they had always drunk. They were unaware that God's river test had begun. Gideon didn't say a word. He gave no instructions. He quietly reached into the water, cupped his hands, and drank. Only 300 men looked to their leader before they drank from the river, cupped their hands, and drank the way he did. They passed the river test.

Whether we realize it or not, all of us are standing at the river's edge, on the verge of a test. Our leader is Jesus. We have the Holy Spirit to teach us and guide us into all things. The Bible tells us to imitate those of faith and to imitate God. So we must imitate our leader, as Gideon's men imitated him, to be able to defeat our enemies and emerge victorious in the trials and challenges of life. We do this by pursuing our leader with zeal—with a driving thirst for more. The Bible commands us to pursue the Kingdom of God passionately and single-mindedly. There is no lower gear that pleases God and obtains the prize. The book of Hebrews says that to please God, we must have faith. It defines this as believing that He exists and believing that He is a rewarder of those who diligently seek Him (see Hebrews 11:6). Unfortunately, most people, including many believers, feel that energetically pursuing the Kingdom of God is excessive, wrong, and even frightening. As I said before, they are uncomfortable when people love Him with all their strength.

When I met the Lord, I committed to being zealous for God wherever I went and with everyone I spoke to. What soon amazed me was how people, Christians in particular, tried to get me to settle down and be "balanced." But Jesus was not balanced at all—He single-mindedly did only what He saw His Father do. No wonder people were threatened by His lifestyle and teaching. He was the zeal of God embodied.

I have observed that those without zeal rarely receive anything from the Lord. The thirsty drink differently. They sound different, look different, and are different. I had a strange but instructive experience once while preaching in Galilee, Israel. A Hebrew rabbi was serving as my interpreter, and I spoke to the group in Galilee about how I had once been touched by the very hand of God. My experience was like Paul's on the road to Damascus. With one touch, I became a different person.

My interpreter did well relating my English words in Hebrew, at least at the beginning. He was fiery and firm in manner. Then the power of God seemed to increase with the preaching, and conviction began to hit the Israelite crowd. But a dynamic kicked in—as the conviction increased, the interpreter's agreement with what I said decreased. He had started out forcefully, but as the anointing flowed into the room his voice became soft. I continued to preach with passion, but the stronger I got, the weaker he got.

Finally, as I was about to invite people to receive and welcome the power, presence, and glory of God in the way I had experienced it, my interpreter's voice lowered to a whisper. By this time I was shouting, yet his voice had all but disappeared. I looked over as if to ask, "What happened to you?" But I could see what had happened. His religious training had taken over and was ruling him, causing him to lose his voice completely. He was physically unable to repeat the anointed words God was speaking.

Fortunately, by that time language meant nothing. Crowds of people rushed forward in spite of the lack of interpretation, and they experienced the anointed power of the Spirit. Those people drank the message of God, while the interpreter refused to drink, though all were in the same place. In the same way, churches are full of people who drink half-heartedly or not at all. The fallacy of church growth is that people think if they can get a crowd in a building, they have a big, successful church. Just remember that 10,000 men went down to the river to drink, and God selected just 300 of them—the ones who drank well.

It's not who drinks, but how you drink. And how you drink has a massive impact on everyone around you.

Take our kids, perhaps the most important people around us. They closely watch how we drink and often pattern their behavior after ours. Yet I've seen plenty of people bring their children to church, thinking that the *where* will overpower the *how*. How the parents drink is worldly, and the children cannot be fooled. Though these parents force their kids to be quiet and look straight ahead in the pew, putting on the disguise of reverence, the parents then steal glances at their watches or phones, and the children can tell they're bored and don't want to be there.

How you drink tells your kids everything they need to know about what you believe. Dragging kids to church will make things no better and may make things worse. Non-thirsty parents may attend church to be with friends and associates or to give their children a religious upbringing, but kids are not persuaded by lack of thirst and lack of submission to the Lord's example. On the other hand, if you are thirsty and drinking in such a way as to demonstrate that you've chosen to follow Jesus' pattern, your child will want to develop that thirst and way of drinking too.

So how do we become thirsty when we are not? How do we cultivate desire when we feel no desire?

To use a kind of embarrassing example, when I was in my thirties, I noticed I started gaining weight. I suspected it was because I drank regular Coke. When someone suggested I switch from Coke to Diet Coke, I decided to give it a try. At first, the diet version tasted awful, but I continued to drink it. Days passed, and my taste buds adjusted. One day I tried regular Coke out of curiosity, and to my surprise, it tasted awful! My palate deemed it far too sugary. My appetite had changed. (And changed again—I've realized since then that diet drinks are not that healthy for me, either, so I've made the switch to unsweetened green tea.)

Therein lies the answer for how to change our appetites. Drink what you want to become thirsty for. Don't wait for the feeling to come upon you. If you want to become thirstier for the things of God, the answer is simple: Drink more of God. The more of God you taste, the greater will be your thirst for more. At the same time, your appetite for worldly things will shrink.

Are you thirsty? How do you drink? The answers to those questions—and what you choose to do with those answers—will tell you everything you need to know about your level of satisfaction and vibrancy in God.

12

SURVIVE THE SIFTING

Not Everyone Is Positioned to Advance

STEVE GRAY

As I study the remarkable events of Gideon's life, from his cowering in the winepress to his achieving complete victory over the Midianites, I wonder—as you may wonder for yourself—where I fit into the story. Which person would I be? Of course, we'd all like to be a Gideon, a hero. Yet the hard truth in this account is that most people apparently won't choose to be like Gideon or the 300 men chosen to accompany him on this divine mission.

Think about it: 32,000 fighting-age men met at the river in all, and all but a relative handful were sifted away. While the story of Gideon is exciting and offers hope that average people can become heroes, the reality is that the majority, at least according to this account, will be sifted out as unsuitable for battle.

Living a Life without Options

How do we survive God's sifting? It may surprise you that there are practical things we can do to get on the right side of this very real Kingdom process. One of those things was demonstrated for us by those who trembled in fear and headed home, when given the opportunity. Of 32,000 men, 22,000 trundled off into obscurity. Gideon and 10,000 men stayed, to their credit. We can learn from them and do what they did to survive that first level of sifting. The reason they succeeded is that they gave themselves no option.

If you want to survive the sifting of God, live a life without options. Others may hold onto backup plans, or the options to quit or back down or change their minds—but not you. To be a person God can depend on, you must take every option off the table. Once you choose Jesus, options cease.

Kathy and I started out in a traveling ministry. For seven years, in a made-over Greyhound bus, we drove from city to city ministering in churches. Then a sifting began. In this new season, traveling from church to church seemed off the mark and out of place. So we headed home to park the bus and try to hear from God. Now we had no income, and we still owned a home and two cars. A sifting had begun.

Sifting can be challenging—I would guess it always is—but it is meant for our good, giving us the chance to demonstrate our level of faith by walking with confidence in God, in spite of external factors or pressures. Without anywhere to go, I was left with plenty of time to seek God. One day while alone in prayer, I felt a strong impression from heaven. God drew my mind to the story of Mary and Martha. The two sisters were at home, and Jesus, their guest, was teaching. Gathered there were other people who were listening to the teaching and needing to be fed. Martha was busy in the kitchen, as she always was when there were guests. Normally, Mary would have been there too, helping get the meal ready—but not on this day. Instead, Mary went in and sat with the men at Jesus' feet, in the position of a disciple. Women weren't disciples in those days, at least not alongside men in the same way. Yet Jesus didn't rebuke her for breaking from the cultural norm. Mary had taken a bold step and found herself on the right side of God's will.

Sister Martha did rebuke Mary and openly complained about her not helping serve at an important moment. Rather than agreeing with Martha and shooing Mary into the kitchen, however, Jesus approved of Mary's choice. He also pointed out the truth of Martha's heart—that she wasn't just worried about the meal, but was anxious about many things.

As I felt God impress this story on my heart, I replayed the choices of the two women in my mind. Then I heard this: *I am giving you a choice. No matter what you choose, I will love you just the same. You can spend time in the kitchen with Martha, or you can spend time at My feet, like Mary. What do you choose?*

I knew what the Lord meant by His application of this passage to my life. The kitchen represented busy churches, already well established and feeding people. If I wanted, I could serve in one of those churches as a pastor. The other option—sitting at the feet of Jesus—meant in my case serving as a pastor in a tiny town, in a sagging, rickety, 150-year-old church. It had been closed for the last four years, had no people and no money, and badly needed new paint.

It didn't take me long to make the choice to be a Mary instead of a Martha. I chose to be sifted out of what might be called "mainstream religion," into what turned into a wilderness experience at Jesus' feet. To me, it seemed the obvious choice, not that it was easy. But it led to a great revival that I'm sure never would have taken place had I chosen the more predictable, "safer" option. As I said before, all sifting is designed for our advancement. Sifting is ultimately meant to do us good.

The problem, if there is one, is that God is not the only one doing the sifting. Think of the time Jesus turned to Peter, called him by his former name, and said, "Simon, Simon, Satan has asked to sift all of you as wheat" (Luke 22:31 NIV). Wow, that's not good. But in the next moment, Jesus prophesied that Peter would survive that sifting to become a leader of his apostolic brethren and of the fledgling Church: "But I have prayed for you, Simon, that your faith may not fail. And when you have turned back, strengthen your brothers" (verse 32).

That's a promise to all of us that when we're being sifted, Jesus is on our side. He's not only praying for us, but He sees ahead, to the greater future for which the sifting is preparing us.

Why Sifting Happens

Sifting can happen for several reasons. One is to hold you back from a task because of your present lack of faith. God sifts some out of the action, just as He did the 22,000, not necessarily as punishment, but because there is a lack of faith to carry out the task.

God may also sift, or allow sifting by Satan, to test us and demonstrate our loyal commitment to Him and His will. This is for our encouragement, to show us to ourselves.

At other times, God sifts us out of ungodly relationships, wicked attitudes, or worldliness. In each case, He has our best in mind, even though at times it may seem as though we find ourselves sifted away from our preferred direction.

The example of Gideon speaks loudly to us, if we allow it to. He followed God's instructions for the sifting of his fighting men, and he never gave himself the option of quitting or refusing to be the leader God needed for the victory. He was cautious and made sure he was hearing God correctly—who can forget his double-verification test with the wet and dry fleeces? He also certainly questioned his own strength and ability, but in all of it, he never gave himself the option to pull the rip cord and bail out on God's will.

Implementing a No-Options Lifestyle

A practical way of implementing living a life without options is to have what my family calls presets. Plainly put, this means three things:

1. There are some things we always do.
2. There are some things we never do.
3. There are some things that are up for discussion.

Our family goes through life with presets. We have "always dos," "never dos," and things "to be decided." For instance, we always go to church. There is no tension on Sunday mornings while we decide what we as a family will do. We're going to church. That decision has been made for life. It's easy.

Another "always do" is that we always tithe, giving a minimum of 10 percent of our gross income. We've done this for the last forty years and will continue to do it, because it's a preset. It's not up for discussion anymore.

In the same way, we always serve. We die to ourselves. We always keep our word, because God keeps His. We never regard helping when needed as an inconvenience. It's something we always do. All these things, and many more, are preset.

By the same token, there are some things we never do. Our "never dos" include these: We never hate. We never throw tantrums. We never use the word *divorce*. We never stop loving God. We never stop loving each other.

Among other benefits, presets remove stress and help keep us safe. Stress results from always having to make decisions. Presetting our behaviors, attitudes, and lifestyles removes stress because most things in your schedule and in the realm of your attitudes and emotions have already been decided. Presets liberate us from doing dumb and harmful things, and they save us a lot of time and the needless concern that arises from making the same decisions over and over again.

In the third category of presets are those things that need to be discussed. I remember when my daughter was in high school and all her friends were really into watching movies. This was back in the day when you had to drive or walk to the video store, rent a DVD, and return it when you were done. Watching movies didn't fit into the first two categories of our presets. I couldn't say that we always watched movies, like many who have stumbled into an entertainment addiction. Yet we did watch movies sometimes. Movies, then, were "up for discussion," based on how we allocated our time and the content of the movie in question. That's just one example of something that falls into the gray area, and we found those discussions to be good and healthy for us as a family. It demonstrates that you can sift your own life by the choices you make. It's a very powerful thing to do.

Sifting Ourselves by Our Choices

King Saul, a once-great man, sifted his life by his own doings. Saul was told that in an upcoming battle, he was to annihilate the enemy. No person or animal was to remain alive (see 1 Samuel 15:1–3). Saul went into battle and won, but when the prophet Samuel met him, perhaps to congratulate him, Samuel suddenly stopped in his tracks. Something wasn't right.

"I have carried out the LORD's command!" Saul claimed (1 Samuel 15:13 NLT). I picture him with a big grin on his face, expecting the man of God to pat him on the back. But Samuel, slightly confused, asked (in my paraphrase of verse 14), "Then why do I hear sheep bleating and cows mooing—and why is this foreign king still alive?"

Saul has a perfectly good explanation, as everyone always does: "The soldiers brought them from the Amalekites; they spared the best of the sheep and cattle to sacrifice to the LORD" (verse 15 NIV). But that wasn't in obedience to the Lord's command. Saul had sifted himself out of power by his own actions, and God rejected him as king.

This reminds me of a phrase we used when I was in my late teens and early twenties and worked at the carnival for part of the summer. When a customer threw a dart at balloons, or tossed a ball at milk jugs, and missed, the carny in charge of that game would shout, "Close, but no cigar!" A cigar was literally the prize at times, which I'm guessing is where the saying came from. But no customer won by getting close. You had to hit the target—or no prize.

When we're being sifted, close isn't good enough for God. Saul won the battle—that was good—but he didn't follow God's orders for what was to happen after that. His example is sobering, to say the least. Our culture has become so lax in serving and obeying the Lord that, like Saul, we may not even seem to realize we're missing the mark. The fear of the Lord has been replaced by the fear of being perceived as a fanatic. Fanatics go too far. They are super-dedicated to God but lack the balance that "normal" Christianity provides—or so it is said. But, like King Saul, are we justifying our failure to obey what God says?

Comfy Christianity reminds me of a bunch of people playing air guitar. They swing their arms windmill style and scrunch up their faces like rock stars getting after a solo. There's only one problem: There's no guitar. No notes issue from any strings. No musical creativity is involved, though there can be plenty of theatrics. Paul used a similar example from his day, a boxer who swings his fists in the air in the presence of no real opponent and pretends to gain victory (see 1 Corinthians 9:26). How many believers seem to be fighting, or playing air guitar, yet are achieving nothing and producing nothing? How many people around us are living moderate, comfortable, balanced Christian lives, even as they are being sifted away from the work within the Body of Christ that God intended for them?

Even Moses, one of the greatest men to walk the earth, the man who led the children of Israel from slavery, parted the sea, witnessed the miracle of manna, and so much more, was sifted. As a result, he didn't get to enter the Promised Land. It began early in the journey, when water was needed. Moses struck a rock with his staff. Water flowed out freely. But fast-forward forty years, and water was needed again. God told Moses to speak to the rock this time, but Moses was upset at the people. He called them rebels and yelled, "Must we bring you water out of this rock?" (Numbers 20:10 NIV). Like before, Moses struck the rock—not just once, but twice—and again water flowed freely.

The problem was, God had told him to speak to the rock this time. By instead hitting it twice, Moses sifted himself right out of entering the Promised Land. God could have overlooked Moses' misstep, but it hadn't happened in private. Moses had flagrantly disobeyed the Lord's command in public, with all eyes on him. Close wasn't good enough. Moses engaged the rock and got water to come out, but he didn't do it the way he was told to.

How careless we become, hoping that "close" will be close enough for God. When our spiritual preset is firmly on lukewarm and our light is set to low beam, it's so easy to miss what God is looking for. How many siftings are we failing day after day?

Sifted Out Because of Fear

As we saw in the account of Gideon, fear is the reason most people falter in their sifting. What started as an army of 32,000 was sifted down to 300, largely because the cowards were invited to go home and 22,000 were happy to oblige. Have you ever experienced an overwhelming dread that made you want to run away from a particular battle? Maybe a termination notice from your boss landed on your desk or in your inbox. Maybe you learned that your child is flunking out of school. Sometimes even the ordinary pressures of life mount up until, overcome by anxiety, we're tempted to turn tail and run back home rather than stay in the ranks.

Fear sifts people out of their callings—fear of man, fear of rejection, fear of change, fear of the future, and even fear of death. Fear connects you to the enemy, while faith in our commanding officer, Jesus, keeps us plugged into all the power, authority, and victory that flows from the Kingdom of God. There is no in-between choice. We operate either in fear or in faith, and God sifts us to reveal which one is at work. Our enemies today are not the Midianites, but we are in a spiritual war. "For our struggle is not against flesh and blood, but against the rulers, against the authorities, against the powers of this dark world and against the spiritual forces of evil in the heavenly realms," Paul wrote in Ephesians 6:12 (NIV).

For those who walk by faith, fear is never an option. Others may live with the option to give in, quit, back down, or change their minds, but to be the person God can depend on, we must be like Gideon and take every option off the table. Again, once you choose Jesus, options go away.

I'm reminded of the parable of the ten minas (see Luke 19:11–27). A mina was a form of currency. In the parable, a nobleman planned to leave the country. He called his servants together and gave them each ten minas, with instructions to invest the money. When the nobleman returned, one servant had earned him ten more. That servant was put in charge of ten cities. Another servant had made five more and was put in charge five cities. A third servant was afraid and didn't invest at all; instead, he hid the money. The nobleman became angry and took from that servant what he had, giving it to the one who had made ten more.

These men had been sifted. The lesson they learned is clear and important. Two did what was right and followed directions. One man, because of his own fear, didn't obey. As a result, he ended up with nothing—and here we find the indicator that tells us if we have been sifted away from opportunities God wanted us to engage in. Let me explain, and I'll begin with a couple of questions: Are you frustrated and feeling as if something is missing in your life? Are you haunted by a sense of purposeless and aimlessness?

Those feelings may be right! They may indicate that something that was intended for you may have gone to someone else.

You may have been sifted like the 22,000 who were sent home to live their normal lives. While others are out fighting exciting battles with epic results, you are stuck in a seemingly humdrum existence.

Sifting Yourself toward Opportunities

The good news is that you can get back to what God has planned for you. Gifts, abilities, and assignments are changing hands every day. Some people accept them; some reject them because of the sifting. If you stay submitted and faithful, follow instructions, get your presets right, and imitate those of proven faith, then what someone else has squandered today might fall into your lap tomorrow.

I believe Gideon would say, "Just follow the directions exactly as given." His story teaches us the value of courage, faith, and trust in God's plan, despite our own initial doubts and fears. Gideon needed a lot of encouragement, but then he followed God's command and led his army to victory over the Midianites. This story truly demonstrates that even the most ordinary person can accomplish great things if he or she trusts God and steps out in faith.

If lack of purpose and lack of hopeful expectation characterize your life, come back into alignment with God. Create some presets for your family and yourself. Remove options from your life in areas where God's will is known. Then see what God can do with you. Those who make themselves fully available enjoy the most adventurous and fulfilling lives. Sift yourself toward the opportunities God wants to extend to you. Like Gideon, you will see that willingness and obedience make all the difference in the world.

PART 3

CARRYING

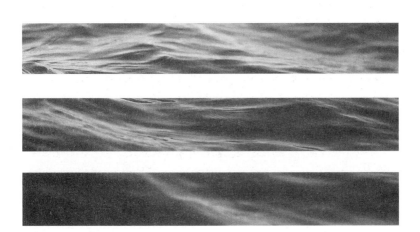

13

THE *NOW* MOMENT

Heaven Moves Faster Than We Imagine

STEVE GRAY

One night, God spoke to Gideon: "Get up and go" (Judges 7:9 isv).

Immediately, Gideon obeyed, going down to the camp of the Midianites and listening to what they were saying. He arrived just in time to hear them discuss a dream and its interpretation, which predicted that the entire camp of the Midianites would fall into Gideon's hands (see verses 13–15). This information gave Gideon an extra boost, but only because he went when God told him to go. Had he hesitated, he never would have heard what the Midianites were saying.

Gideon responded without hesitation to God's "*now* moment." But for centuries, right up to the present day, Christians in general seem to have been set on slow speed. The concept of reverence has come to look like doing things ploddingly. When God is depicted in a movie or a play, notice that He never speaks fast. In every case, the creators make His voice low and slow. When a Christian says, "Let us pray," our bodies, minds, and mouths automatically slip into slow motion too.

Yet I have found that the Kingdom moves fast. God's movements are deliberate, but not slow. According to the Bible, God's voice sounds like thunder or many waters. Lightning flashes from His throne. Angels travel at the speed of light. The praise of the redeemed is described as almost deafening.

The problem with slow-motion Christianity is that we're more likely to miss our *now* moments. I used to pray for people in the traditional slow and steady way, asking them to form a line, and then going down the line, listening to their needs, and praying for each one before moving on. But when revival hit our church and we were meeting five nights a week, I realized there was no time to do things the way they had always been done. God's power was coming explosively, and all you had to do was be near it to get God's results. *Now* moments were everywhere. Slowness only got in the way.

To respond correctly to the *now* moments of God, we need to change our thinking in a few specific ways. First, we need to understand that God is not locational the way we are. He is not confined to the platform or the prayer line. He is the God of the front row and back row, God of the living room and bedroom. We can grab onto His *now* moments wherever and whenever they arrive.

Second, we need to be fully persuaded in advance so we can respond more quickly. Paul, in Romans 4:21 (NIV), described Abraham as "being fully persuaded that God had power to do what he had promised." Paul said he himself was persuaded that nothing can separate us from the love of God. Persuaded people experience mighty moments in God because they've already made up their minds that God is able to do more than they can ask or think. They don't have to work up the faith; they respond instantly.

If you need to meditate on God's command, analyzing it or sitting on it for too long, you will miss God's *now* moment. *Now* means *now*, not *later*.

Third, we need to free ourselves from the preconceived idea that God is as relaxed as we tend to be. We know God is love. He is merciful; He is kind. But Moses also wrote, "The Lord is a warrior; Yahweh is his name!" (Exodus 15:3 NLT). Ask a hundred people who God is, and no one will answer, "God is a warrior."

What is a warrior God like? Timid, passive, and unassertive? Does a warrior God tiptoe cautiously around? Of course not. So, if God is in warrior mode, how does He relate to me? How do I communicate with Him? What kind of response does He expect from me?

Paul said "we have the mind of Christ" (1 Corinthians 2:16 NKJV). This means our mind should operate like that of a warrior. A warrior's mind is neither passive nor cautious. I have observed that a passive mind is a very dangerous mind. People with passive minds have no power to stop what the enemy throws at them. Whatever thoughts are flying through the airwaves, passive people allow into their heads.

By contrast, the apostle Peter wrote, "Be alert and of sober mind. Your enemy the devil prowls around like a roaring lion looking for someone to devour" (1 Peter 5:8 NIV). How can the enemy devour us? I blame a passive mind. Those with passive minds accept every idea that enters their heads, believing it's from God. We must learn to think like warriors. Thoughts need to be filtered through the Word of God. We don't accept the enemy's propaganda. We are to capture our thoughts and make them obedient to the knowledge we have of Jesus (see 2 Corinthians 10:5). People with passive minds are easily devoured because they haven't trained their senses to discern between good and evil. Their senses are like an open ditch. Whatever is flowing at the time gets in.

Having the Mind of Christ and Using It

God wants us to use our minds so we don't miss our *now* moments, but some renewing must take place. Romans 12:2 (NIV) says, "Do not conform to the pattern of this world, but be transformed by the renewing of your mind. Then you will be able to test and approve what God's will is." I've often taught that if you want to change how you act, you must first change how you think. I appreciate the fact that Paul boldly told the Corinthians we have the mind of Christ. But as we all know, having His mind and using it are two different things.

I learned a valuable life lesson about this many years ago that I still reflect on today. A woman minister in her eighties took me under her wing. She was a unique woman with a unique past. For one thing, she had been born blind and was completely healed of her blindness. She also was a woman of revival. During the 1950s, her church was open twenty-four hours a day, seven days a week, for five or six years. The people were experiencing many signs and wonders, particularly healings.

One day while I was in this minister's home, a young lady who worked at the church burst into the room and wanted to know what to do about this or that. The eighty-year-old spiritual warhorse began to tell her what to do. The inexperienced young lady interrupted her to say, "Aren't you going to pray about it?"

The older woman looked right at her and said, "Why? I have the mind of Christ."

I never forgot that lesson. The mind of Christ knows the will of God, and with that mind, I can know it too. Yes, the Holy Spirit may speak to us and give some specific direction, but if He does not, we still have the teaching of Scripture to tell us how to think. We aren't passive thinkers, but active thinkers and speedy doers.

Gideon's *now* moment led to a similar moment for his entire army. God was dressed in full armor, so to speak, when Gideon returned to the camp. Gideon shouted the order, "Get up! The LORD has given the Midianite camp into your hands" (Judges 7:15 NIV). Imagine if all but one of the 300 men had jumped up and obeyed, while the one pulled the covers over his head and said, "You guys go ahead. When God tells me personally to get up, I'll be there, right by your side."

Having observed the Kingdom of God at work for these many years and in many different circumstances, I think I know what would have happened. The army would have won the battle, but done so with less favor because God had said He would defeat the enemy with 300 men. Since only 299 showed up, the army was "down" a man. That man's obedience would have carried favor, but because he wasn't obedient and didn't grab his *now* moment, the army was deprived of his share of strength.

The lesson for you and me is simple: The born-again spirit is always ready. The born-again spirit will always say yes to God. Your spirit is ready *now* to "get up and get going." When the church needs volunteers, the born-again spirit says yes. When you hear about a person in need, the born-again spirit says, "I'll help." Your born-again spirit never says no to God's commands—but you are more than a spirit. You are also a mind, with a will and emotions locked up in a body. This creates inner conflict when the born-again spirit is saying yes to everything spiritual, but your will or emotions want something else. Jesus described it this way: "The spirit is willing, but the flesh is weak" (Matthew 26:41 NIV).

For Gideon's implementation of God's plan to work, he needed 300 men to respond to their *now* moments. That's just what happened. Gideon divided the army into three groups of 100 each and instructed them to do exactly as he did, at the same time. Together, in their proper places, they reached the edge of the enemy's camp. With the Israelites' trumpets blaring, jars breaking, and torches blazing, the Midianites turned on each other with their swords. *Now* meant *now*, and it worked. The Midianites ran, crying aloud as they fled (see Judges 7:16–21).

Being Get-Up-and-Go People

Here's a basic truth: The enemy never runs crying when confronted by a passive mind. The Body of Christ and the world need get-up-and-go people today. It's hard to get people up for the battle when their goal is to relax, retire, and do nothing. If there's ever the opportunity in your life to experience God's divine power and presence, it will require you to respond to your *now* moment and get up and get going.

Now moments don't last. They come, and then they go. In John 4:35 (NIV) Jesus said, "Don't you have a saying, 'It's still four months until harvest'? I tell you, open your eyes and look at the fields! They are ripe for harvest." The disciples were giving themselves more time to get started, but their timing was off. Jesus said the harvest was ripe right then. Too many Christians give themselves more time, and by the time they finally decide to get up and get going, God's moment is gone.

The consequences of missing God's timing can be more than just lackluster church services or a boring prayer meeting. They can be deadly. Jesus prophesied Rome's destruction of Jerusalem, which took place in AD 70: "They will dash you to the ground, you and the children . . . because you did not recognize the time of God's coming to you" (Luke 19:44 NIV). How often has God visited our nations, our denominations, our churches, our families, or us personally, but we did not recognize it? Then, when trouble comes, we get confused and wonder, *Where is God?* The fact is, He was here, but then the *now* moment passed, and as prophesied, our enemies took His place.

We need *now* moments today if we're to demonstrate the victorious Kingdom lifestyle to the world. Without such moments, we're left talking about what God did and what God will do, and we miss His moments today. Preachers often preach about the past. Preachers also preach about the future. But what about now? Jesus is "the same yesterday and today and forever" (Hebrews 13:8 NIV). What is He wanting to do right *now*, in this moment?

Creating Our Own *Now* Moments

The account of blind Bartimaeus always puts a smile on my face. Every day, Bartimaeus sat by the road begging. When he heard that Jesus was passing by, he shouted, "Jesus, son of David, have mercy on me!" (Mark 10:47 NIV).

Many rebuked him for shouting, but he shouted even more. Finally, Jesus stopped and said, "Call him" (verse 49).

It appears that Jesus could have kept on walking, but Bartimaeus had created his own *now* moment. So the bystanders told him, "Cheer up! On your feet! He's calling you" (verse 49).

You know what that makes me want to do? Call out to Jesus right now, saying, "Son of David, have mercy on me! Have mercy on us! Have mercy on my family, my church, and my nation!" I have faith to believe that Jesus will hear my words, turn, and call me to Himself, working a miracle.

The entire world seems to be worn down. For many, even for believers, life's joy is in short supply. We could really benefit by hearing, "Cheer up! On your feet! He's calling you." But that begins when we call out to Him without giving up. We actually invite God's *now* moments by demonstrating our desire and readiness to respond.

John Wesley famously said,

. . . the devil himself desires nothing more than this, that the people of any place, should be half-awakened, and then left to themselves, to fall asleep again. Therefore, I determine, by the grace of God, not to strike one stroke in any place where I cannot follow the blow.[1]

Frank Bartleman, a prayer leader in the Azusa Street Revival, declared,

Opportunity once passed, is lost forever. There is a time when the tide is sweeping by our door. We may then plunge in and be carried to glorious blessing, success, and victory. To stand shivering on the bank, timid, or paralyzed with stupor, at such a time, is to miss all, and most miserably fail, both for time and for eternity.[2]

Do you hear the call to get up and get going, and act in some area of life, for some good work? Don't let a passive mind slow you down and keep you from laying hold of the *now* moment that is surely available to you.

14

UNITY BRINGS VICTORY

What God Is Up to Is Bigger Than You

▌ STEVE GRAY

"Do you not know that your bodies are temples of the Holy Spirit, who is in you, whom you have received from God? You are not your own" (1 Corinthians 6:19 NIV).

We are not our own. Gideon's 300 men were not their own either. Why did Gideon separate these 300 who drank with cupped hands from the 9,700 who didn't? It wasn't to identify bravery or some other personal quality. It wasn't because they were the same height and strength. It didn't even matter that there were specifically 300 of them. What mattered was that they were unified. The Midianites didn't flee because of the courage of this small army of men; they fled because that army acted as a single unit.

Unity brings victory. Yet the Body of Christ has lost nearly all semblance of unity today, and as a result we are mostly fractured and powerless.

Drive through any town in America and you will see church after church after church, all of them Protestant. The word *Protestant* comes from the word *protest*, which is fitting. Martin Luther protested some of the practices of the Catholic Church more than five hundred years ago, and the Protestants have been protesting ever since. By contrast, in my hometown of about twenty thousand people, there were two Catholic churches, one on the east side of town, the other on the west. Both did things the same way. A Catholic can attend church anywhere in the world and know exactly what will take place and how to participate. The Catholics have conformity down pat. Protestant churches—of which there are at least two hundred in my hometown—are like that proverbial box of chocolates. You never know what you'll get.

The proliferation of "protesting" churches tells me that rather than striving for and achieving unity in a local body, Christians usually prefer leaving when they don't like something. They start another church where everyone conforms to what they believe. In doing so, they reject the diversity from which true unity derives. This is why, in my view, Western Christianity places great emphasis on personal salvation and personal growth in Christ. We aren't looking for corporate power, but individual expression. So we rarely achieve signal, history-changing victories like the one Gideon's army achieved.

I remember that one time during our travels, Kathy and I were given a lovely suite at an upscale hotel. Not only did we have a private pool; we also were given a private butler. He was our personal butler, not shared with anyone else. We could contact him day or night. Unfortunately, many Christians view Jesus that way, as their personal Savior on call twenty-four hours a day.

The problem is that the Bible doesn't describe Jesus as our personal spiritual butler. He isn't even described as our personal Savior. Rather, He is called the Savior of the world. Salvation is usually referred to as a group reality. Each person must decide to participate or not, but once a person decides to belong, then

Christianity becomes a team sport. Paul wrote to Timothy, "Join with me in suffering, like a good soldier of Christ Jesus" (2 Timothy 2:3 NIV). The concept of a soldier works because we understand that when a soldier joins an army, he loses his individuality. Heads are shaved, and everyone is given an identical uniform. For an army to succeed, each person must see himself as part of the group.

Confusing Conformity with Unity

In my first year of college, I joined the Reserve Officers' Training Corps, or ROTC, for a year. This was back in the day when students were protesting the Vietnam War, and respect for law enforcement and the military were at a low point. Because of that, I didn't really want to pursue officer's training; I just wanted cheaper college tuition, which was given to ROTC members.

I didn't fit in well with the group. In those days, my hair was shoulder length. The army didn't approve of that, and to stay in the program they said I had to have short hair. This became a problem for me and the guys I hung around with, who also had ample heads of hair. To solve the problem, we applied grease to our hair every Tuesday and Thursday afternoons when we were required to put on our uniforms and march. We packed down our manes and hid them under our hats. My first captain discovered this and gave me an F for my first semester. After that, I joined the ROTC band and played every event possible on or around campus and got to keep my hair long. I was given an A for participation, and at the end of the year it all averaged out to a C. Not bad for a semi-rebellious college student in the 1970s.

In those days, the US government was drafting fighting-age men to go to Vietnam. I was listed as 1A, meaning I could be in the next group. One day, I got a government letter. *Oh boy*, I thought, *here we go*. But the letter stated that the army had filled its quota for the year, right up to the number before mine, and I would no longer be considered for the draft. That was music to my ears, because had I gone to Vietnam, I would have gone as a second lieutenant, which is a platoon leader and the most dangerous role in the army. Even though I wasn't a Christian at the time, I believed that my avoiding the war was a God thing.

In retrospect, being in the ROTC illustrated some spiritual principles to me. For example, the army was trying to build unity, but instead required conformity. I might grease my hair, or even cut my hair, to conform to the ROTC system, but I was in no way unified with that system or its officers. Religion behaves the same way, confusing conformity with unity. You've probably seen groups like the Amish, which may or may not have internal unity. But they do have a high level of outward conformity, all wearing old-style clothing, driving horses and buggies, and living without modern conveniences. One time, I met members of a different religious group that mandated that no member could own anything shiny, such as jewelry or even a chrome bumper on a car. To conform to this rule, members painted their shiny automobile parts like handles, wheels, and bumpers black. That achieved conformity, but not necessarily unity.

Gideon wasn't looking for conformity. We know nothing about what his men wore or if they were tall, short, or similar in any way. What Gideon needed was unity. He needed a group that would respond instantly and trustingly when given an order. Armies are like sports teams. To win in sports, players must set aside their individual identities and come together as one unit. If a player plays for himself, he is derided as a selfish showboat. Showing off individual skills brings shame and shows a group's weakness. Unity brings victory.

Diversity Required

On the other hand, though it may sound paradoxical, to be strong, unity requires diversity. Consider the example of Peter, the lead apostle, who was a Jew and who struggled at first with accepting non-Jews into the Christian fold. Eventually, Peter learned to accept that non-Jewish Christians possessed equal rights and privileges within the Church. They didn't need to become Jews, but rather they joined together with Jewish Christians to create strong unity within the Kingdom of God.

This unifying process was a challenge for Peter, and I'm sure for some others in the early Church. He was in the habit of eating at a table with both Jews and non-Jews—until some out-of-town Jews showed up. Peter realized that these Jews would not accept his eating with non-Jews, so after their arrival he moved to a Jews only table to avoid any criticism. But Paul, also a Jew, saw it and was furious—so furious, in fact, that he spoke up in front of everybody and exposed Peter's hypocrisy (see Galatians 2:11–21). Why, Paul wondered, if we live by faith, would Peter and others separate from Gentiles, who also lived by faith? In the Body of Christ there are not two tables, but one table for us all. In other words, there is unity among diverse family members.

Paul was pointing to the great strength of the Body of Christ—that it is made up of all kinds of different parts, just like the human body. Therein lies its wonder and its power. But, like Peter, we often try to separate ourselves by outward distinctions, cultural backgrounds, even music preferences. I drove by a church not far from where I live and saw a sign that read, "Traditional church, 8:30 a.m. Contemporary church, 9:30 a.m. Mixed, 10:30 a.m." What is this—made-to-order church? How sad that we can't meet in unity with diversity. Instead, many churches today offer services that conform to a narrow range of personal tastes. But unity means being one in spirit, not necessarily one in outward things.

When Kathy and I opened the doors of a church in Smithton many years ago, we had to ask ourselves, Why are we doing this? Did anyone really need another church? The answer to us was obvious. Nobody needed another church that was just like every other church. But what about a different kind of church? What about a church where everyone was born again? What about a church where everyone was filled with the Holy Spirit and spoke in tongues? What if everyone, including children, praised with lifted hands? Could we have a church where everyone loved God, and the length of the service didn't matter? Years later, here in Kansas City, anyone can come to a service and see exactly that kind of church. There is no conformity. Your past doesn't matter. Clothes don't matter. Age doesn't matter. What matters is what God likes. We unify around what He wants. We don't cater to anyone's personal preferences.

Personal preferences were a non-issue in Gideon's army. It didn't matter if some guys didn't like the sound of trumpets. It didn't matter if others preferred a sunrise battle to a middle-of-the-night battle. What was needed was the instant, focused, get-up-and-go unity of the spirit that would follow God's directions through Gideon. In a similar way, if our goal today is to push back the powers of darkness so we can dwell in safety and prosperity, then personal likes and opinions only get in the way. What matters is how God is leading us as a body. Amos 3:3 (NIV) says, "Do two walk together unless they have agreed to do so?" To walk with God, we must agree to do so on His terms. We must dedicate ourselves to making the Holy Spirit comfortable in our midst. Our goal is to create a church that God attends. People are important, but personal preferences too often keep a church divided.

The key to victory is a unity that welcomes diversity. We shouldn't resort to church splits where one group breaks away from another because people can't handle diverse customs or personalities. Paul wrote in Ephesians 4:3 (NIV), "Make every effort to keep the unity of the Spirit through the bond of peace." He fought hard against everyone aiming to become the same. Gentiles don't need to become like Jews to maintain the spirit of unity; neither do Jews need to become like Gentiles. What we must become is the same in the Spirit. We do not become alike. We become unified.

The Yoke of Unbelief

Paul wrote in 2 Corinthians 6:14 that we are not to be unequally yoked with unbelievers. Unfortunately, unbelief may be the yoke that holds people together more than we care to admit. Most sermons I hear on being unequally yoked pertain to dating and marriage. But we can be yoked to family and friends, allowing our decisions and preferences to be influenced by them rather than by the person of Jesus Christ. Marriages, families, home groups, churches, and denominations can be held together by decisions, actions, and values contrary to those of Jesus.

One of my favorite ways to demonstrate that unity brings victory is the story of Joshua at Jericho (see Joshua 6). Yes, the walls of that great city did come "tumbling down," but what caused such a miraculous event? God had a plan, and it went like this:

Part 1: March around the city once, all the armed men together, for six consecutive days. (The key was getting the men to do this, along with seven priests willing to carry trumpets out in the open, in front of the Ark.)

Part 2: On the seventh day, all march around the city seven times, with the priests sounding the trumpets.

Part 3: Then, when the priests sound a long blast on the trumpets, the whole army—meaning everyone, without exception—give a united shout, and the walls will come down.

Part 4: Everyone go straight in.

As it was with Gideon's 300 men, so it was with the army at Jericho. God gave no room for personal preferences or opinions. There wasn't a vote. They didn't get to choose their instruments, or the number of times they walked around the city, or any other aspect of how God's plan would work. Rather, they had to act completely in concert with one another. It required a unified army, with no exceptions. There would be no power in partial participation. Only "the power of all" would bring the walls down.

Fast-forward to Acts 2. The same lesson applied. We assume there were 120 assembled in a room, because in Acts 1 it says the group numbered about that many. The writer of Acts tells us that among the crowd were women, the mother of Jesus, and His brothers. But about this 120—in more than one place in the Bible, we're told that after His resurrection, Jesus appeared to as many as 500 at one time. My question is, Where were the other 380 who saw the resurrected Jesus? Why weren't there 500 in that meeting place?

We can only speculate, but in light of what we're talking about, it could be that the missing 380 had legitimate-sounding distractions like a busy schedule, or else they were afraid of being seen with the disciples. We'll never know. We just know that when the Day of Pentecost had fully come, 120 were all together.

Suddenly that day, a violent wind blew and tongues of fire rested on all of them. All were filled with the Holy Spirit, including Jesus' mother and brothers, and all spoke in other tongues. This is a clear picture of unity leading to power. The Bible says they were all together, they were all filled, and they all spoke in tongues. Why can't we have a church like that, where the power of all is present as it was then?

One reason is that modern Christianity caters to numbers, not so much to unity. When the goal is to grow a church numerically rather than in unity, the result is a mixed group, with some people really engaged, a lot seemingly disengaged, a few great worshipers in the pews, two or three dancers in the aisles, and rows of rebels, halfhearted hearers, and back row backsliders. Churches like that don't resemble an army, but a rabble.

The key to unity of spirit amidst diversity of various kinds is that we hear and agree on what God is doing right now. Gideon gave us a vivid picture of this. At the right time, his army shouted, blew their horns, and broke the jars containing torches. Joshua and his army pictured this unity of spirit as well. Unified, they marched around the city exactly as God told them to, shouted at the trumpet's sound, and went straight in, over the crumbled walls.

What if that were the goal of each church? To hear God clearly enough together that we know when to raise a shout, when to sing, jump around, bow in reverence, sit quietly, listen to teaching, and so on? Can you imagine the power of a group of believers unified in the spirit and responding as an army, with instant obedience? That's the picture God gives us through these armies of Gideon and Joshua—and it's a reality available to us corporately, if we will commit to go after it.

Inner Unity

The born-again spirit is not a rebel. What I mean is, the spirit of a born-again person always agrees with God and is in complete unity with Him, ready to say yes or no in obedience to His direction. This simple fact is an ongoing encouragement to me. If there's a conflict inside me, it's not with God. It's the fleshly, untrained body that wants to control things. As Paul says in Galatians 5:17 (NIV), "For the flesh desires what is contrary to the Spirit, and the Spirit what is contrary to the flesh. They are in conflict with each other, so that you are not to do whatever you want."

I know from personal experience, as I'm sure you do, that my born-again spirit will not voluntarily back down, but neither will my flesh. Both want to win, and both will fight desperately to win. To be caught in the middle is a frustrating existence. We become double-minded and unstable in all our ways (see James 1:8). Many believers seek psychological counseling to understand why they are unhappy or confused. Often, nothing is wrong with such people. They are just experiencing the same battle we all face between the carnal flesh and the born-again spirit. They know what's right and what God wants, but they also want to live for themselves.

This internal battle is the most miserable when neither side wins. God prefers a victory—any victory—to a stalemate. He is no friend of the tepid and wavering. In Revelation 3:15–16, Jesus said He prefers that we be hot or cold; the lukewarm He will spit out of His mouth. Joshua was right when he declared, "Choose this day whom you will serve" (Joshua 24:15 ESV). We all have the same choice, and not choosing is choosing. To attempt to avoid choosing is itself a choice to walk in the middle of the road, the wide way. It's an attempt to sit on the fence and remain comfortable—which always produces lasting discomfort instead.

Some think choosing God's will is difficult. But choosing not to follow your born-again spirit's desire is worse. Paul taught that if we sow to please our fleshly nature, we will reap destruction (see Galatians 6:8). We each get to choose, but some choices are deadly and destructive to our walk with God, and to each other. This is what I taught my kids as they reached their upper teen years, whether they were still living at home or were away at college. When they would find themselves entangled in some struggle or decision, I would tell them, "You can do whatever you want." They would look back at me in shock. Then I would tell them what I thought would be the right thing to do with their freedom to choose, and then I would add, "Ultimately, it's up to you."

This lesson remains true for each of us throughout our lives. You can do whatever you want, and no one can stop you. Yet your choices are not free. You will reap something. From the spirit, you will reap the spirit. From the flesh, you will reap destruction. "Don't mock God," Paul urged us all. "You will reap what you sow" (my paraphrase of Galatians 6:7).

After becoming a Christian, what I had sown before became evident. From my middle teen years onward, I hadn't answered to anyone. I could do whatever I wanted all the time. I didn't think in terms of right or wrong. I had no moral compass, and I based all my choices on me, myself, and I. Then, at the age of twenty-three, I gave my heart to Jesus, but my former life choices remained costly. They included an attitude that believed, *If it feels right, do it.* That motto made it seem that everything was permitted and beneficial, if it didn't hurt anyone. But it did hurt someone. It hurt me, and I had to learn to follow my new leader, Jesus.

Free will isn't free. It can cost you relationships, friendships, money, positions, and, most of all, your own peace of mind. When in a battle, Christians often claim to be fighting the devil, or fighting with unrighteous people. Battles can give that appearance, but most of the time we're fighting an internal battle with ourselves. This inner battle with ourselves is ongoing, and victory can be gained, lost, and regained. Your spirit and will are warring to achieve unity with the Holy Spirit so that you can become powerful and effective. The world doesn't have to change for you to gain this victory. Your friends, spouse, kids, or job may stay the same, but everything about your life will change when you get the upper hand in the inner battle. Unity, inside and out, matters to God because it brings victory.

15

ACCESSING THE GOD ADVANTAGE

Understanding the Reality of Favor

STEVE GRAY

An angel told Gideon, "The Lord is with you, mighty warrior" (Judges 6:12 NIV). We know God is everywhere, but this announcement shows that God's presence also comes to people in specific, empowering ways. It is the ultimate advantage, giving even the least and weakest of us power to overcome anything in life's battles. Money, position, fame, prestige, resources, and connections cannot assure victory. But the God advantage—the advantage of His presence—will bring you triumph every time.

This was how Gideon rose to a great challenge, with only 300 men carrying jars, torches, and horns. God's presence gave him the ultimate advantage over the vast Midianite army. It proved the ultimate weapon that assured victory. Having the God advantage redefined Gideon's life, and it will redefine yours too.

The Land of Drawing Near

While in slavery to Egypt, the Israelites were given the land of Goshen in which to live. *Goshen* means "to draw near." There, God drew near to prosper and protect the Israelites from harm. God's space and Israel's space overlapped, so to speak, so the Israelites experienced the God advantage. Living there, they grew large in number and strong in body and mind. In Goshen, they escaped the plagues of Egypt.

The God advantage remains available today. The minute a person fully believes, the God advantage kicks in and eternal life begins. Protection arrives. Faith in the redeeming blood of Jesus the Messiah, shed on the cross, shields our lives from the influences of sin and death. The God advantage covers and fortifies every person who draws near through Jesus.

I've noticed that the God advantage doesn't adhere to conventional expectations. It often brings promotion to a person who doesn't appear to be next in line. Doors of favor swing open to unexpected positions of influence and authority. As "the head and not the tail," individuals with the God advantage experience a divine elevation that defies human logic (Deuteronomy 28:13 NLT).

Kathy and I have always desired to take the message of revival to Israel. On one trip, we brought with us a couple of other pastors and some students. The students didn't own any luggage, so we loaned them our extra set. Then we prepared them to go through Israeli airport security, which can be somewhat intimidating. We encouraged them to be honest and forthcoming. So when the students were asked if the luggage they had was their own, they said no. This was true because it belonged to us, but when the security clerk heard their answer, it set off a firestorm of questions.

The Israeli airline staff split Kathy and me up for separate interrogations and took the students somewhere else. Our belongings were scattered everywhere, and they lobbed question after question at us to see if we all gave the same answers. Finally, a young, female supervisor who appeared to have just graduated from high school brought our group together. She turned to me and asked, "Why are you going to Israel?"

"I'm a pastor of a church in Missouri," I said. "After so many years of trying to do God's will, I found myself exhausted by trying to get everything right. Then, after hitting the lowest point in my life, I walked into my church, and with everyone watching, I was struck by the power of God. It was like the glory of God descended on me."

As I continued to describe what had happened to me, I saw tears streaming down her cheeks.

"Shouldn't that be happening in the Holy Land?" she asked.

"Yes, and that's why I'm going to Israel," I replied.

She raised her arms and shouted, "Then come on through!"

That story brought the God advantage into that uncertain moment and opened the door for us to Israel.

On our most recent trip there, Kathy and I traveled as guests of the government. We were met at the airport by several people who escorted us to a private vehicle, and we were driven around to get our baggage. Then we were driven to the president's home and briefed on new security measures the government was putting into motion. Later, we met with Isaac Herzog, who is now president of Israel, and discussed the future of Israel.

They then drove us to a highly secure air force base, and to our surprise, we were invited to sit in the cockpit of a sophisticated surveillance jet. On the tarmac next to the plane, two soldiers, one male and one female, explained the dangers of each mission. I prayed with them, asking that the God advantage would remain over them.

"From now on, every time you fly, remember my words and believe that the favor and protection of God is on your lives," I told them.

Their faces showed that no one had ever prayed the God advantage over them before—and that they were open to receiving this higher form of power.

Miracles and Triumph

In moments of adversity and crisis, the God advantage breaks addictions that defy human strength, mends relationships, and makes crooked paths straight. This divine intervention brings miracles and healing, offering hope and a path forward, even in the most challenging circumstances.

Those who possess the God advantage are recipients of divine favor and become conduits of God's goodness, love, and mercy. Having this advantage will increase your harvest financially. It reaches into all broken areas of life, offering restoration to minds clouded by doubt, marriages strained by trials, families torn by discord, and relationships scarred by pain. In embracing this advantage, believers will find their lives restored by the transformative work of a loving and present God.

Before becoming local church pastors, Kathy and I traveled with a great ministry team for about seven years. On a trip to Reading, Pennsylvania, it was just Kathy and me, along with my mother, who was a great minister in her own right. On a stretch of highway some ten miles from Reading, our bus just quit. No motor, no lights, no steering, no nothing. All I could do was pull over to the side of the road.

We called a tow truck, which towed the massive vehicle to a nearby repair shop. People from the church in Reading came to pick us up, and we gathered what we could and went on to do a service that night. The next morning, I was up early and went out to the repair shop where the bus was waiting to be serviced. The guys at the shop were helpful, but said they were all booked up and wouldn't be able to look at it until the following week. Seeing that we needed it sooner, they offered to let me hang out there and use their tools to try to repair it myself. They kindly offered to answer any questions I wanted to bring them.

All day, I inspected, poked, and prodded the vehicle until it got so late that I had to be picked up for church that night. The next day, I was back in the repair shop, doing the same thing. I asked the mechanics for advice, and occasionally one would step outside and look at the bus with me and try something. But after two days, the mechanics were stumped and so was I, and our ministry team remained stranded.

Back to church I went, and though the bus was dead, the services were alive and on fire. In fact, intense prayer for the resurrection of our bus was going up at the church and among friends across the country. But the next day, I don't know why I even rode out to the repair shop again. The situation seemed hopeless, and I was out of options. The bus sat there like a metal corpse, apparently ready for the junk pile.

Sometime that afternoon, I just stood by the side of the bus, staring at it as you would a dinosaur skeleton in a museum. There was a two-lane, tree-lined frontage road behind the repair shop that ran adjacent to the interstate. Without hearing or seeing anything beforehand, I turned to see that an old, red pickup truck had pulled up, apparently on that road, and a thin man of about retirement age had gotten out and was walking over to me.

"I can tell you what's wrong with your bus," he said. "Go tighten up the ground connection in the battery compartment."

I didn't question his advice, for some reason. After I had been analyzing the situation and trying solutions for three days with professional mechanics who couldn't fix it, why would I think this guy from nowhere had the magic solution? Yet it didn't occur to me to ask. I simply opened the battery compartment, grabbed a small wrench, and gave the wing nut half a turn or so. I didn't take time to close the compartment, but rushed to the driver's seat, pushed start—and immediately the engine fired right up.

What happened next was even stranger. I turned to look out the window at my newfound friend, but he was gone. Overjoyed at the fact that the bus was running, I practically jumped out the bus door, but there was no older man, no old, red truck. There wasn't even the sound of it leaving. The man and the truck had seemed to disappear.

Baffled but happy, I ran into the repair shop and told the mechanics about the red truck and the man who had helped the bus start right up. Perplexed, they looked at me, not understanding.

"What truck?" they said. "What man? We didn't see anyone."

It finally dawned on me that I had been visited by an angel. I had experienced the God advantage.

Advancing the Advantage

If you belong to Jesus, you have the God advantage right now. Many, however, live with what I call an inactive advantage. Here's what you can do to move into "active" God advantage status: *follow only one God, disentangle, separate, don't neglect*, and *impart*. Let me explain each of these a little further.

Follow only one God: Following other gods is a fatal mistake that has plagued God's people throughout history. The Bible tells us, "You shall have no other gods before me" (Exodus 20:3 NIV). While we may not be tempted to worship a golden calf, we can still be lured away from our devotion to God by false gods like money, fame, lust, addiction, greed, and power. It's important to be honest with ourselves about what motivates us, and to make sure that our love for Jesus and our commitment to His covenant is what drives us each day.

Disentangle: The people we associate with can have a huge impact on our spiritual lives. The Israelites often found themselves entangled in disobedience because of the wrong associations they kept. We must be vigilant about whom we spend time with, making sure that we surround ourselves with people who will encourage us to live holy lives and follow God's plan.

Separate: Holding onto old ways and refusing to separate ourselves unto God is another pitfall. We must actively cut ties with sinful practices and embrace holiness if we want to maintain the God advantage. Some examples of what this might look like include making sure that we're spending time in prayer and reading the Bible every day, and seeking out a community of believers who are also committed to living holy lives.

Don't neglect: Neglecting our spiritual growth is a recipe for disconnection from God's intervention. We must prioritize our faith development and nurture our relationship with Jesus if we want to obtain the God advantage. This might mean getting up earlier each day to spend time reading the Bible, finding verses that apply to our current situation and posting them around our home, and getting involved in a good Bible-believing church.

Impart: Finally, failing to pass on the torch of faith to the next generation can create a generational void that's difficult to overcome. The book of Judges tells us that the next generation of Israelites after Joshua had become lawless and devoid of faith, which led to the need for deliverers like Gideon (see Judges 2:6–13). We must intentionally impart our faith to the next generation if we want to prevent the God advantage from fading away. As parents, pastors, teachers, and leaders, we must all work to pour into the next generation and teach them how to maintain God's advantage in their own lives.

These are some of the ways that you can advance your God advantage status and make sure it stays set on active rather than inactive.

Don't Hesitate!

For the God advantage to work effectively in our lives, we must learn not to hesitate in critical moments. We talked about the importance of *now* moments in chapter 13, where we saw that God's *now* means *now*, not *later*, and that the born-again spirit is always ready to say yes when God says move. When I instantly took the older "man's" advice about the bus, the engine started, and the crippling problem was solved.

Again, having the God advantage brings us victory every time. Don't hesitate to use the spiritual advantage He gives you! Let

His presence cover and protect you, His strength fortify you, and His favor bring you promotion so that you can accomplish all He has for you to do. Because you are His child, the God advantage rests upon you—and it restores, transforms, and empowers every life it rests upon.

16

GOD DISRUPTIONS

Standing Strong in the Shake-Ups

J. D. KING

Unexpected things transpire when God shows up. The status quo is upended. Heavenly breakthroughs are unleashed that catch the eye and arrest the attention. I have witnessed these holy disruptions countless times.

I remember once when the Spirit came down on a group of people in rural Missouri. As they were seeking the Lord, the fire of the Holy Spirit swept over them, and they flew back three feet. It was a clear work of the Lord; no one touched them. I know this claim sounds bizarre, but I witnessed it with my own eyes.

Another time in a prayer gathering, I saw worshipers fall like dominoes—row by row—from the front to the back. As people were collapsing, some were crying and shrieking, while others were shaking. One of the individuals on the floor had been contemplating suicide, but God delivered her from the spirit of death. Others testified how God rescued them from depression, bitterness, and fear. One man said, "I don't think I would have believed you if you told me this is what happens. In fact, it might have even frightened me, but now I don't want to leave."

Unusual experiences transpire as people encounter the glory of God. On one occasion, a couple receiving prayer began behaving as if they were intoxicated. It was like the time in Acts when Peter said, "These men are not drunk as you suppose" (Acts 2:15 ISV). I've witnessed seekers so inundated by the Lord's presence that their speech was slurred and their legs were wobbly. Some had to be carried out to their cars because they were so overwhelmed.

One night, a couple was overcome by the Holy Spirit and had to be helped out of the building. On their way back to the hotel, some police officers pulled them over. They made both the man and the woman take a breathalyzer test and walk a straight line. The authorities didn't believe that this couple was experiencing the effects of a God encounter. Yet with no evidence of alcoholic intoxication, they had to release them.

As you can imagine, not everyone appreciated what was going on in these gatherings. A journalist from the *Word & Way*, a Missouri Southern Baptist periodical, visited the meetings and published a report titled "Slain in Smithton." Although mostly sympathetic, the article did question people collapsing under the weight of God's glory. The journalist quoted Dwain Carter, a Baptist pastor who visited the outpouring services. This minister said, "The worship, the music, and the sermon were excellent." He was uncomfortable, however, with individuals falling back while receiving prayer, and insisted, "The Bible says when you encounter God, you fall on your face.'"[1]

Throughout history, people encountering the glory have crumbled to the ground in a myriad of different ways. As the Spirit moved, some fell on their faces. Others collapsed backward. I've even read accounts where people fell to their sides. The distinctions that this Baptist minister highlighted are virtually nonexistent in the annals of history.

As the Holy Spirit draws near, there will often be a shaking "so that what cannot be shaken may remain" (Hebrews 12:27 NIV). I've watched the Lord do this kind of thing in restaurants, parking lots, and living rooms. God shows up in all sorts of places. I've seen people impacted at a movie theater and at a swimming pool. The glory of the Lord can come into all sorts of spheres. One time, I had to help someone get his car out of a ditch. He was so overwhelmed by the glory that he veered off the road.

I know this sounds extreme, but the Lord is still shaking whatever is shakable. We hold too tightly to the frivolous things. In a move of God, certain signs can attract outsiders and simultaneously reveal the callousness of insiders. Inexplicable wonders can force people to grapple with difficult questions. As the saying goes, sometimes God offends the mind to reveal the heart.

When God Disrupts

During the time of Gideon, the Lord used unconventional methods to achieve victory. God moves in mysterious ways, disrupting popular belief. In the era of the judges, armies relied on weapons like swords, spears, and slings. Using torches and shofars with only 300 men was not considered a viable strategy. I don't think any other military force at that time would have attempted that kind of maneuver. God, however, is a disruptor who zigs when everyone else zags.

> It was just after midnight, after the changing of the guard, when Gideon and the 100 men with him reached the edge of the Midianite camp. Suddenly, they blew the rams' horns and broke their clay jars. Then all three groups blew their horns and broke their jars. They held the blazing torches in their left hands and the horns

in their right hands, and they all shouted, "A sword for the LORD and for Gideon!"

Each man stood at his position around the camp and watched as all the Midianites rushed around in a panic, shouting as they ran to escape. When the 300 Israelites blew their rams' horns, the LORD caused the warriors in the camp to fight against each other with their swords.

Judges 7:19–22 NLT

The long blasts of the shofar unleashed sounds that the Lord used to disrupt the enemy. Through the refracting light of the Lord, the Israelites' torches burned more brightly and conveyed a holy fire. Within these disruptions, the supernatural overlapped with the natural, subverting everyone's perceptions. When God showed up in power in the Midianite camp, agitation arose, and the enemies of Israel turned against one another.

In a single night, 300 men defeated the armies of Midian and their allies, who "had settled in the valley like a swarm of locusts," with numbers so vast that their "camels were like grains of sand on the seashore" (Judges 7:12 NLT). This small company of Israelites conquered a vast army without touching a weapon. The inexplicable acts of God always bring awe and wonder.

A Whole Lotta Shaking Going On

When the Lord breaks into our lives, it isn't always easy to understand. I recently received a call from a young man who is extremely sensitive to the things of the Spirit. Scott and I had discussed what it meant to be receptive to God, and he had really been growing.

As we talked, Scott told me he kept trembling and feeling overwhelmed. He was unsure about what was going on, and he wanted prayer. I asked him whether anything had coincided with the onset of the shaking. Scott revealed that around the same time, he had received distressing news about a close family member. This person's life and marriage were spiraling out of control.

I asked Scott if it was possible that the Lord had given him the burden to intercede and stand for this relative, who had fallen out of the church and didn't have much support. Maybe the Lord was calling him to pray.

As it turned out, this was precisely the case. God was trying to grab Scott's attention and have him stand in the gap for his family member. The trembling was calling him to a deeper place. Sometimes, there's something very meaningful happening when we are overwhelmed. The Lord might be shaking you out of a stupor and pointing you in a new direction.

Idealized Notions of Outpourings

God often breaks into history, disrupting the natural order of things. Though common, it's still a challenging experience for many. I've met thousands of Christians who embrace religious forms but deny the Spirit's power (see 2 Timothy 3:5). So many talk a good talk but leave little room for God to intervene.

People say that they want fiery worship experiences, but they clearly don't want things to get disruptive. They want powerful moments, but hope those end by noon on Sundays. Religious folks want the fire to fall, but only if it fits into their delicate sensibilities.

Shockingly, some of the loudest advocates for a move of God will oppose it as it emerges. Historian Arthur Wallis wrote, "There are always some who are desirous of revival until it comes, and then they bitterly oppose it because it has not come in the way they anticipated."[2]

Outpourings of the Holy Spirit are often romanticized in books, so people develop an idealized notion of what those look like. If a gathering doesn't seem to check off every box, naysayers are therefore quick to dismiss what's transpiring.

Many have a hard time imagining that God would work through imperfect vessels. Evangelist William Alexander McKay declared, "Do not despise the great river because of the sticks and straws that may occasionally float on its surface."[3] It's easy to criticize the blemishes and the rough edges, but it takes maturity to appreciate a holy treasure housed in earthen jars.

Holy Knock-'Em-Down Power

Throughout history, when the Lord has moved in the lives of people, things may have gotten messy. Not everything the Lord institutes in people's hearts fits neatly into our modern religious boxes.

As time passes and stories are retold, they get told differently. The unbridled fervor in the earliest days of a revival is an integral part of a movement's legacy, but these parts of the story are often left out of later accounts.

The Second Great Awakening (1801–1830), for example, was raucous. One observer said "people screamed until you could hear them for three miles on a clear night, and until the blood vessels stood out like whip cords."[4] An evangelist said he saw women "throw themselves back and forward with such violence, that they threw the combs out of their hair, and then their loosened locks would crack nearly as loud as a common carriage-whip."[5] The work of the Spirit in this era was sometimes referred to as a "holy 'knock-'em-down' power."[6]

Unusual bodily responses also transpired during the Welsh Revival (1904–1905). Evan Roberts, one of the key leaders, claimed that God "filled his soul with divine awe," and as he fervently interceded, "every member of his body trembled until the bed was shaken."[7] God shocked many believers in this move.

Similar outworkings transpired in the Hebrides Revival (1949–1953). As the Spirit of God moved across the windswept Isle of Lewis, some responded in an unusual way. Duncan Campbell, one of the leaders of this awakening, shared the following:

Physical manifestations and prostrations. . . . I find it somewhat difficult to explain this aspect, indeed I cannot; but this I will say, that the person who would associate this with satanic influence is coming perilously near committing the unpardonable sin.[8]

It may come as a surprise, but the moments when people met with God were usually characterized by extraordinary phenomena. So, modern evaluations must be made with a measure of humility. D. Martyn Lloyd-Jones, who pastored Westminster Chapel in London, once asked, "What do we know about these great manifestations of the Holy Spirit? We need to be careful 'lest we be found fighting against God,' lest we be guilty of 'quenching the Spirit of God.'"[9]

Moves of God are often untamed, characterized by things that are difficult to understand. When we as believers try to discern these things, it's important to avoid hasty judgment. We need to be open to the unique ways God operates. If we aren't careful, we might find ourselves fighting against Jesus. That would be awful.

Unusual Phenomena in Scripture

When discussing God disruptions, it's vital to draw understanding from Scripture. As always, the Bible is our source book and guide. We need to let it speak.

For instance, the priests of Israel, during the reign of Solomon, were overcome by the glory of God while serving in the Temple. According to Scripture, "The cloud filled the temple of the LORD. And the priests could not perform their service because of the cloud, for the glory of the LORD filled his temple" (1 Kings 8:10–11 NIV). God's servants were paralyzed.

The prophet Ezekiel also experienced the overwhelming "glory of the LORD" later, and relating his encounter, he testified, "When I saw it, I fell facedown" (Ezekiel 1:28 NIV). Despite being a mighty man of God, the seer was humbled as he encountered the Lord's splendor.

Daniel, a courageous man who stood his ground against lions, was also brought to the floor in the overwhelming glory of the Lord. When encountering this, he lost all strength and his face turned white. In his own words, he declared, "I had no strength left, my face turned deathly pale and I was helpless. Then I heard him speaking, and as I listened to him, I fell into a deep sleep, my face to the ground. A hand touched me and set me trembling on my hands and knees" (Daniel 10:8–10 NIV).

In the first century, the Temple guards attempting to capture Jesus were also mysteriously struck down. John recorded this unusual episode, writing, "When Jesus said, 'I am he,' they drew back and fell to the ground" (John 18:6 NIV).

The apostle Paul also collapsed in the dirt as he came face-to-face with the Lord. Luke recounted in the book of Acts, "Suddenly a light from heaven flashed around him. He fell to the ground and heard a voice say to him, 'Saul, Saul, why do you persecute me?'" (Acts 9:3–4 NIV).

Finally, John the Revelator describes his overwhelming experience with Jesus. What he witnesses brings him low. He writes, "His face was like the sun shining in all its brilliance. When I saw him, I fell at his feet as though dead" (Revelation 1:16–17 NIV).

When God's glory breaks into the room, it has a transformative effect that can upend lives. Throughout history, individuals have had profound experiences that have altered their outlook and faith. Such phenomena are not limited to the biblical era, but continue to unfold in our world today. How God has operated in the past gives us a hint into how He operates today.

Leaving Room for the Inexplicable

Not everything can be scientifically measured. Holy Spirit phenomena can be particularly confusing to Americans, who view the world through a highly rationalistic lens. Many of our friends and neighbors struggle to comprehend the meaning of intense spiritual experiences. Our compartmentalized, scientific outlook dismisses feelings, touch, and invisible heavenly realities. Westerners seldom see reality as accurately as they imagine. They only see part of the picture.

Moves of God are filled with intense, passionate encounters, but are much more than mere emotionalism. According to John Wimber, a prominent voice in the 1980s and '90s, Americans formulate "laws" for all aspects of life, ranging from medicine and physics to philosophy, psychology, and economics. This tendency often leads people to dismiss things that cannot be scientifically measured. Many appeal to "rationalism to explain away the supernatural."[10]

Our worldview shapes what we perceive—and what we're inclined to ignore. When we embrace a reductionist approach, we filter out experiences that cannot be explained by scientific methods alone. It's therefore important to adopt a more open-minded perspective and recognize the limitations of some of our measuring sticks. God is much bigger than the boxes we try to put Him into.

The Bible makes it clear that there is more in the cosmos than what humanity can categorize or provide analysis for. Not all that exists can be easily harnessed. We must always leave room for the inexplicable.

Outward Signs of Inward Works

How the invisible affects the visible is difficult to grapple with, and this can be even more challenging during a move of God—when heaven and earth almost seem to overlap.

A colleague and I recently discussed some of the unconventional responses that occur during seasons like this. While my friend acknowledged the notable effects that God's power has on people, he questioned whether all their responses were caused by God.

I told him that while God can directly move on people, it would be a mistake to think that this is always what is occurring. Most responses during a revival are human reactions to the work of the Lord. John Wesley, the Methodist firebrand, argued that they were "outward signs, which had so often accompanied the inward work of God."[11] They were merely an indirect sign of heavenly activity. Not all that people do has a direct correlation with a move of God, but where there's smoke, there's often fire.

In an era dominated by skepticism toward spiritual realities, it's crucial for believers to acknowledge the extraordinary works of the Lord. By humbly giving Jesus the benefit of the doubt, we acknowledge the limits of our own understanding. Cultivating a receptive attitude toward the Lord creates space for Him to move in and around us.

No Place for Resistance

When we encounter God, things get shaken up, and it's important to let God do what He will. Manifestations or bizarre displays should never be our focus, but it's vital to remain open to the ways God operates. As believers, we must leave room for the diverse manifestations of the Holy Spirit, even when they surpass our understanding. Let's not be disheartened by the mysterious nature of these workings, but rather move to embrace them fully.

Your responses matter. Whether you like it or not, a person's reaction in the face of extraordinary displays reflects his or her faith. The biblical story of Peter walking on water illustrates this point. Initially, Peter stepped out of the boat and walked toward Jesus on the water. When he noticed the winds and the waves, however, fear overtook him, and he began to pull back (see Matthew 14:29–30). Shockingly, many believers find themselves in a similar place of resistance when facing something as immense as a move of God.

In Acts 8:39, the Holy Spirit transported the evangelist Philip several miles. This extraordinary event wouldn't have taken place if he weren't willing to submit to the Lord's mysterious hand. Resistance to the Spirit hinders the work of God. That's why people often see more miracles in developing nations than in the West. The people from those nations are less opposed to the possibility of the supernatural. Most foreigners aren't like rationalistic Westerners; they are mindful of the realm of the Spirit.

Of course, God is sovereign, and He can do whatever He wants. Nevertheless, He often chooses to work through willing people. Whenever His agents refuse to align with Him, it undermines the protocols of the mission. Only those who cooperate with the Lord will be able to venture into the deeper waters of revival.

Let's not be hindered by resistance or fear. Let's instead yield to the Holy Spirit's work. Believers shouldn't be afraid of God disruptions. We should embrace the Lord's works with an open heart and a willing spirit.

Regarded Too Much; Regarded Too Little

While some charismatic believers may place undue emphasis on strange phenomena, most Western Christians seem to have no grid for such things. They dismiss anything they don't understand. I know several Christians who have asked if we really need any of this at all. They don't accept things that are out of the box, or approaches that might offend modern sensibilities.

John Wesley grappled with this issue generations ago. He offered some poignant words:

> The danger was to regard extraordinary circumstances too much, such as outcries, convulsions, visions, trances, as if these were essential to the inward work, so that it could not go on without them. Perhaps the danger is to regard them too little; to condemn

them altogether; to imagine they had nothing of God in them, and were a hindrance to his work.[12]

Wesley urged believers to use their discernment as they encountered unusual manifestations—neither idolizing nor disregarding them. It isn't easy to get this right. On the one hand, I have friends who are always talking about unusual phenomena. They have an unhealthy obsession with bizarre displays. But on the other hand, I have colleagues who are dismissive of most everything. They leave no room for mystery. I had a friend who asked me which was worse. I told him it was difficult to answer that question. Both extremes can get out of hand. But if I had to choose, I would rather have wildfire than no fire at all.

Of course, "everything must be done decently and in order"— but believers mustn't forget that the Lord is still saying that "everything must be done" (1 Corinthians 14:40 HCSB). Not appreciating a particular manifestation or approach doesn't mean you get to sit on your hands.

I don't have all the answers on how churchgoers should work through all these things, but I know that an openness to the Lord is vital.

Opening Our Lives to Divine Disruption

Throughout history, figures like Gideon, Jesus' disciples, and the intercessors during revival eras experienced the mysterious works of the Lord. As a result of such encounters, these men and women gained remarkable insight, becoming instrumental in catalyzing changes all over the world.

During a move of God, heavenly disruptions upend the established order, leaving an indelible mark on people's lives. Suddenly, the invisible becomes tangible. Those caught up in the majesty and glory see things they never saw before. I can assure you that whenever the Lord shows up, nothing remains as it was. Everything becomes new!

We need to open our lives to the inexplicable wonders of God's Holy Spirit. We need to make room for Him in our morning commutes, our dinner table conversations, and everywhere else we go. The invisible needs to break into the visible and shake things up. Are you open to that? Will you let the glories of heaven disrupt your life?

17

SUSTAINING GOD'S PRESENCE

What Does It Take to Keep the Fire Burning?

| STEVE GRAY

"Throughout the rest of Gideon's lifetime—about forty years— there was peace in the land" (Judges 8:28 NLT). The sound of the trumpets blasting and jars being smashed didn't die out in a day, or even a year. That miracle reverberated through the next forty years, and an entire generation lived in peace because of one man's obedience and faith. That is a picture of God's sustained presence in a community—and it is exactly what He intends you and me to experience today.

I remember in the early 1980s hearing about a church in Kentucky that was enjoying an outbreak of the power of God. By the time I was made aware of the meetings, they were in their sixth week. The thought of six continuous weeks of revival almost overwhelmed me. I couldn't attend the meetings because of our ministry schedule, but I made sure I got the recordings. I listened over and over, trying to imagine what it would be like to participate in a long-lasting move of God.

Some years later, in the late 1990s, I learned firsthand what it's like to live in God's sustained, reviving presence in my own personal life, and corporately in our church. Kathy and I were given the privilege of not only attending, but leading the Smithton Outpouring revival, in which we held meetings five days a week for 182 weeks. Every week, people from many other states and faraway countries packed that rural church building to encounter God.

When we moved to Kansas City the revival didn't stop, as some predicted it would. Rather, the glory went with us. We met in multiple churches for a time, and eventually we raised up a tent on our current property while the construction of a permanent building began. The presence of God continued, without wavering. When the 9/11 attacks took place, airports closed and people seemed afraid to travel even by car. Crowds stopped coming, but the presence of God never lifted. We continued experiencing His remarkable presence as a local congregation.

Over time, I watched as other fires of revival sprang up in various places around America and the world. After a few weeks, however, most of those burning fires subsided into little more than glowing embers and smoke. People wondered, Is it possible to sustain God's presence for longer than a few weeks, a few months, or even a few years? Many bought the religious myth that revivals cannot continue perpetually, that all good things must come to an end. That belief was promoted even by those who had experienced great moves of God. As a result, it stole the faith of some who could have attended. They viewed what we were experiencing as leftovers from former days, rather than a fresh move from heaven. But those who did visit or join our fellowship experienced real revival, especially compared to what they were often getting back home.

To this day, God's reviving, sustaining presence remains among us, even as we have stopped meeting on Saturday nights at the church and have added home groups, and as we teach on a variety of "non-revival" subjects having to do with things like relationships, finances, and raising children. Yet I am still asked, "How do you keep explosive praise and worship, and strong, full participation in your local congregation?"

It would be easy to answer simplistically, "It's a God thing." The truth is, it is a God thing, but it's also a people thing.

What I mean is this: Each of us can do certain things to sustain the presence of God, personally and corporately. Indeed, we must.

What's Your Treasure?

Whether or not we gain and sustain the presence of God goes back directly to what we treasure. If you want to locate your heart, look at what you hold most dear. Jesus said in Matthew 13:44 (NIV), "The kingdom of heaven is like treasure hidden in a field. When a man found it, he hid it again, and then in his joy went and sold all he had and bought that field."

According to Jesus, the Kingdom is like a hidden treasure a man found and hid; then he bought the field where he hid it, so he could obtain the treasure. Notice that he bought the field. Today, I'm not sure the parable would read the same. Instead, the man would probably find the treasure in a field, walk off with it, bury it in his yard, and then take it to the pawn shop to sell for extra money. In other words, he wouldn't sacrifice to buy the treasure; he would steal it out of a sense of entitlement.

In the same way, many believers don't know how to treasure God's presence these days, because most of us were sold a something-for-nothing gospel. Jesus did everything, and we need do nothing, we've been told. We call it grace, but it's not biblical grace. And because we give nothing for it, we don't seem to value it.

This is not the biblical concept of grace. Grace in that time meant that someone who had little received unmerited favor from someone who had a lot. The person receiving grace was expected to reciprocate by serving his or her benefactor loyally. In fact, the receiver became responsible for speaking high praises about the benefactor's generosity and declaring the person's greatness at the city gates, among the elders. That was the prevailing idea of grace in biblical times. If the person receiving the benefactor's gift of grace didn't honor that person—or worse yet, dishonored him or her—grace came to a halt. Grace was a two-way street, with differing but important commitments on both sides.

In Jesus' parable, the man didn't just take the treasure from the field. He sold all he had to gain the field and the treasure. To this man, nothing was worth more than the treasure he had found. He would stop at nothing to possess it. He gave sacrificially of himself to obtain it. Today, anyone who gives it all as a result of receiving God's grace is seen as trying to add to his or her salvation. Worse, such people are labeled radical, unstable, overzealous. The standard has dropped so low that now we praise Christians who are just a little less carnal than all the others. These "heroes" try a little harder and do things like avoiding the worst movies and music. The problem is churches are not experiencing sustained moves of God. The reason is simple: Jesus must become the treasure we value above all things. His grace is not cheap. It costs us something—in fact, it costs us everything.

I was in a massive revival service at another church one time in which the intensity of the crowd was remarkable. I stood up during the worship time and shared about how I had been touched by the very hand of God. This testimony stirred the people even more, and the hunger to experience God's touch became so strong that as I rushed into the crowd, masses of people—thirty, forty, fifty of them—collapsed under the weight of God's glory. After that unique moment, people lined up at the platform to share what had happened to them. It was an amazing corporate experience of the presence of God.

Then came time to take the offering. The pastor of the church got up and seemed unable to comprehend that God was working in a fresh way in the hearts of his own people. He began to speak and declared, "This is all well and good, but I'm here to tell you today, it's all about souls. It's all about winning souls for Christ." He repeated this a few times, and whenever he would say the word *souls*, he would get a little quiver in his voice, which sounded more dramatic. The effect was as though a thief had entered the room and robbed everyone of what God had just done.

I appreciate the man's desire to share the Gospel with others, but he didn't treasure the move of God taking place right before his own eyes. What we fail to value will not be sustained. It's not difficult to welcome and live in the presence of God, but we must place the highest worth upon it. If Jesus is not our ultimate treasure, I can tell you that the presence of God will not come and will not stay.

Grace Says *No*

A big part of valuing God's presence means developing a strong *Yes*—and a stronger *No*. Serving Jesus most of the time is a *Yes* experience. We say *Yes* to Him as Savior and Lord. We say *Yes* to Him baptizing us with the Holy Spirit. We say *Yes* to speaking in tongues, just as they did in the Bible. We say *Yes* to any assignment the Holy Spirit gives us.

But to sustain God's presence in our lives, we must also put the word *No* to good use. I have never been fond of the word *No*. I especially don't like being told, "*No*, you can't do that," because then I want to do that very thing. Paul explained that he only wanted to covet after God said coveting was not allowed. We all have that same reaction. For example, I'll be doing fine with food, until someone calls a fast. Then all I want to do is eat. *No* is a powerful word that can cause desire to flare up within us.

But to sustain the presence of God, we must take control of the word *No* and use it as a proper tool in God's Kingdom. Paul wrote in Titus 2:11–12 (NIV), "For the grace of God . . . teaches us to say 'No' to ungodliness and worldly passions, and to live self-controlled, upright and godly lives in this present age."

Many get their *Yes* right but can't say *No* to themselves, and so they falter. Worldly passions win because our *No* is weak, and we adapt to a Christianity where ungodliness is tolerated.

How God Thinks

To sustain something from God, we must think the way God thinks. But in many ways, we put our own spin on His thoughts, robbing them of sustaining power. Here's one example: God's Kingdom is a world where the guilty go free. This is the wonder and inestimable value of salvation, yet I have heard some great preachers teach that believers are declared not guilty in Christ. I understand that line of thinking, but it's an inadequate explanation of God's legal system. Worse, it causes us to place less value on salvation, rather than more.

Let me explain. The Bible says that all have sinned and fall short of the glory of God (see Romans 3:23). The apostle John says that if we claim to be without sin, we are liars, and the truth is not in us (see 1 John 1:8). So in God's legal system, we are all guilty. When you put your faith in Jesus, does God take you, a guilty person, and declare you not guilty? Absolutely not. To declare you not guilty would be a lie. You are guilty because you have committed sin, like the rest of us.

But while we are guilty, someone named Jesus paid for our sins. Therefore, we, the guilty, get to go free. This is the greatness of our God. We will always be guilty in the legal sense because of what we did, but we have been granted freedom. Crimes against

God must be paid for. Jesus paid the price for our crimes, and we go unpunished. That is truly amazing grace.

I remember talking to a woman after preaching as a guest in her church. She said, "I always feel guilty after you preach."

I said, "Really? What did you do?"

She looked puzzled. I explained that guilt is not a feeling; guilt is a verdict. The joy of God's legal system is that our rightful punishment has been paid in full for us.

Gideon was guilty, but when he sacrificed to the Lord, his sin was paid for. Notice that salvation is never free. It's only free to me because someone else paid my way. Sin must be paid for by someone.

What does this have to do with sustaining the presence of God? Everything. God's presence is sustained by the value we place on it. Partaking of the tangible presence of God is not cheap. The knowledge that God grants us access to the glory of who He is should remain overwhelming to us. King David pleaded, after sinning with Bathsheba, that God would not take His presence away from him. David understood the value of that presence above all else. We might say it this way: Guilty people enjoy and value the presence of God much more, knowing that only the Father's grace and Jesus' sacrifice make it possible for us to experience it.

Think of it this way: If you ran up a huge amount of debt and couldn't pay it, and then someone learned of this, had pity on you, and wrote a check to cover it all, you would walk around feeling as if you'd been released from prison. Daily, you would remember the outcome you deserved versus the outcome you have. This is the reality of the Kingdom of God. His Kingdom is a debt-free society, and we owe it all to Him.

Living in the Age of Entitlement

In today's culture, however, we don't often see people walking around rejoicing because their lives have been redeemed. Rather, we live in the age of entitlement. People feel entitled to be comfortable wherever they go. They feel entitled to everybody's love and respect, and to their own opinions and feelings. They expect only to be encouraged, and always to be accepted without correction.

But God will not share His presence with those who feel entitled to it. In fact, entitlement is the opposite of how God thinks and how He set up His Kingdom. In God's world, I'm not entitled to anything, while He shares everything with me. In the debt-free system of the Kingdom, no one owes us anything, but we freely receive. Entitlement distorts and ruins the Kingdom dynamic.

I've seen God manifest Himself in many different churches, yet few could sustain it, because a sense of entitlement crept in. I've seen revivals turn corrupt as people begin to feel they deserve more than what they're getting. The irony is rich: Church folks pray to be used by God, and then when God uses them, they get offended because they don't get the recognition they want. People claim to be servants, and then they rise up in pride when treated like servants.

The glory of God is pure, untainted, uncomplicated, and undeserved. In His debt-free society, there will always be a disconnect from His presence if you begin to believe someone owes you something. This goes for interpersonal relationships as well. You will never sustain God's presence personally or corporately if you keep people in debt; that is, owing you something. Consider how each of us holds others hostage in this way. A husband believes his wife owes him more attention. A wife is disappointed because she feels her husband owes her more affection. At work, we feel the boss owes us more money and approval. We expect to be understood and appreciated, no matter what we do or say. We feel entitled.

Do you want to experience the presence of God? Then I encourage you to cultivate the mind I try to cultivate in myself: *No one owes me anything, not even an apology. Nobody is in debt to me. I set everyone free from my expectations and my sense of entitlement.*

This not only increases mutual love and empowers better relationships, but it reminds me that I am a debtor whose debt was paid. God owes me nothing, and neither does anyone else. When I think this way, I find that I'm the one who is set free from the bondages of expectation and entitlement. And I treasure that freedom—and the One who gave it to me.

Uprooting

Jesus said in Matthew 15:13 (NIV), "Every plant that my heavenly Father has not planted will be pulled up by the roots." This is a great lesson for experiencing and maintaining the presence of God. Many attitudes and mindsets have been planted in us by our parents, the culture around us, teachers at church and school, and so on. As much as we like to believe that we are autonomous beings making perfectly unbiased decisions, that's not the case, and Jesus says so. He says some plants need to come up by the roots.

One way to think of this is as clutter that accumulates over time in our hearts and minds. A key to sustaining God's presence is actively to recognize and remove the clutter of things that might not be sin, but also are not part of God's ways. When we value God's presence, we don't sit around and wait for Him to remove the debris. We often know what needs to go. Start pulling those things up by the roots, until zeal for God and His Kingdom outweighs the pull and influence of this world. It will be worth it.

One of the things I most often see cluttering hearts is fear, and this fear keeps people from experiencing or sustaining God's presence in their lives. Paul wrote to Timothy that God did not give us His Spirit to make us fearful and timid; His Spirit provides love, power, and a sound mind (see 2 Timothy 1:7). But I have also noticed that people get over being timid and fearful when they want something badly enough.

For instance, I attended a Kansas City Chiefs football game this year, and it was a loud, energetic experience. People stood up and screamed the entire game, and it was obvious that these people wanted their team to win.

A couple of weeks later, I attended a pastors' prayer meeting. Their whispered prayers made it sound as if they didn't even know what to say. They came across like uninterested people praying for something they didn't really care about. I left that meeting unconvinced that they actually wanted God's presence, or personal revival, or a move of God in their churches. If I wasn't convinced, I don't think God or the devil were either.

People who place great value on a prize, and then go after it, behave and speak in a certain way. You can tell they're convinced. No timidity shadows their words or countenances. They employ the power, love, and sound mind God has given them to obtain the treasure available to them.

Height + Depth = Length

Revival is a powerful force with ebbs and flows, highs and lows requiring the right tensions to sustain them. God showed me this equation: *Height + Depth = Length*. I have found this to be profound.

The height of revival is when God powerfully reveals Himself to people. They are moved, healed, and delivered. The heights give us goosebumps and a sense of awe. I learned this in the first months of the Smithton Outpouring. In the moments after the Holy Spirit swept into our congregation, God so impacted me that I became speechless. The entire congregation was dazed and dumbfounded as well. As their pastor, I thought I should do something. So I moved toward a group standing at the altar. I stretched out my hands toward them. Instantly, they collapsed in a heap. This was no charismatic courtesy drop. It was something new, as if God had cut them off at the knees.

It was a significant change when people collapsed to the floor, but the more significant change was when they got up. They were different. One lady said, "Something happened to me. I feel emotional freedom and love for everyone."

Others shared that the presence of God seemed like a heavy blanket on them. Still others described this time as God doing surgery on their souls.

God revealed Himself to us. It was the *height* of revival. I wanted to shout to the world, "Everyone deserves to experience the presence of God!"

The *depth* of revival is just as important, however. It's where God reveals us to us. In His love, we see our flaws, weaknesses, and selfishness. The depths are a grace allowing us to become better versions of ourselves.

The depth of revival puts a demand on the leader. Preaching cannot only be about God's majestic workings. It also must include a heavy dose of biblical truth to elicit conviction, repentance, reformation, and conformation to the image of Christ. As God revealed us to us in Smithton, people often ran to the front and slid face first, scraping their noses on the carpet. They cried and pounded the floor or lay motionless and helpless as God healed their souls. Hundreds of times, I watched the entire congregation fall to its knees, thanking God for His love. God showing you to you and digging through the layers of unbelief, hurt, disappointment, or failure may sound embarrassing and exhausting, but it is so good and necessary!

After those moments of depth, the Lord would often sweep us again to the heights of His presence. With exuberant praise, our shouts of freedom and transformation could be heard miles away.

Balance is critical, however. Some people, desiring the depth of revival, go too far, constantly dwelling on their shortcomings and failures. Others swing the other way, only wanting the height of revival, without considering the changes that need to happen in us. To sustain revival, we need both the height and the depth, to see God and ourselves in equal measure. When we have this view, we will have the *length* of revival. We will have a sustained experience of God's presence that creates lasting transformation. Revival is not a one-time event, but a continual process of growth and change. When we embrace this process, we can see the continual power of God at work in our lives and in the world around us.

We need to apply the *Height + Depth = Length* equation in our personal lives as well. We must press to go higher and deeper in our personal pursuit of God at home, in marriage, in our parenting, at work, and so on. We cherish the presence of the Holy Spirit—and live like it outside church meetings, where we spend most of our time. We also embrace repentance as a lifestyle, always open to the conviction and cleansing that are chief among the Holy Spirit's activities.

Height + Depth = Length works for congregations—and for each of us individually—as we seek to sustain God's presence in our lives.

God's Presence Is Practical

Experiencing and sustaining the presence of God isn't a miracle. It's a practical, wonderful, achievable lifestyle. Gideon pursued and obtained it. He was elevated from a societal nothing to a war hero. His actions produced sustainable peace. What would it take to make you a war hero on the battlefield of righteousness?

God's sustained presence is not beyond your reach—but to reach it, it must become your all-consuming treasure. It all hinges on your desire. When you want the reviving power of God more than you want anything else, it will become yours. The cure to all of life's maladies, disappointments, loneliness, emptiness, and fear is to discover Jesus as your personal treasure, and to place upon His presence the highest value possible.

What happened to me the night I personally experienced the height of God's presence has been documented, published, and shared. Just the other day, I stood in the doorway of my house, saying good-bye to a new friend. As he was leaving and almost out the door, he turned to me and asked, "What was it like?"

"What was what like?" I asked back.

His eyes teared up, longing to know, yearning to hear put into words the indescribable. There are no words in the English language adequate, but I tried. My friend is an electrician. I asked if he had ever touched a live wire. He had, several times. I told him for me it was like lightning, electrical. This might sound strange, but it was enthusiasm. It was the height of God's deity touching my humanity, and I became a different person in the same body. Yes, I was at church, but it wasn't a corporate experience. It was personal.

I certainly didn't earn the moment. There are steps that got me to that moment. As I look back, experiencing the height of God's presence happened because I wanted it to happen. It wasn't a passing fancy. For me, it wasn't revival. It was survival. I was at the end of me. I didn't want to be me. I didn't know what that meant, but that's how I felt, and obviously God knew it.

I was living the *d* words: discouraged, depressed, distraught, distressed, dejected, deranged, delirious, despairing, despicable, dysfunctional, and desperate. I was lost, with nothing to lose. I had no idea I was going in the right direction. While others were trying to find themselves, I lost myself and found the height of God.

As good as that was, it wasn't over then. God had shown Himself to me. It was time for Him to show me to me. I stood in my garage, praying. The garage wasn't a particularly holy place. It was just that no one ever went out there but me. While standing alone there, I began to see myself. Each time I saw me, I told God what I saw. I didn't hide anything as the list of the me I saw got longer and longer. It wasn't a bad experience or a good experience. It was a necessary experience. It took a while, but then I was done.

Now comes the good part that you might not expect. God's love came into that garage. After I presented a good case of why He should cast me away, God's love, in my ugly moment, filled me like a balloon ready to pop. Who would have thought that I didn't know myself, or would have avoided knowing myself my entire life? God showed me to me, and this time I looked. It was like swimming in the ocean without a life jacket. It feels dangerous, but like Peter walking on water and slipping into the deep, Jesus is there to hold you up. You won't drown in self-loathing. Jesus will be there for you.

Don't Give Up on Height and Depth

I think most people give up too soon on both height and depth. God is so good as to make Himself available to us. It's not always easy getting to Him or getting Him to us. It's not supposed to be easy. If it were easy, it would cheapen the value. God's presence is precious. You must want it more than you want anything else. He is always near, but only a few break through that thin, invisible barrier that exists between heaven and earth.

I am always in height and depth mode. I am always reaching up to Him. I am always looking down at me. I am always aware of God. You can live that way too. Start the journey one step at a time.

Religion is awkward for most of us. We get shy around God and around others pursuing God. So find your garage and start. Better yet, get in your car while in the garage. It will be like a private sound booth. Think about what it would be like to be near God. How good would it be? How badly do you want it?

This is not an overnight trip. You should make plans for taking many days to convince yourself and the Lord how important this is to you. Start with any words you can find to let God know that you want Him above everything else. If you are like most, it will feel as if your words come out of your mouth and fall to the ground, never making it to heaven. Don't give up. Once God is convinced you're serious, your words will land in His court. Height will come.

Next, ask God to start showing you to you. Whatever you see, whatever you feel, tell Him about it. Let Him know you can be trusted with the intimate information the Holy Spirit will show you. Depth will come.

In time, you will be stronger, like a determined Gideon. If God shows you your past, be honest with Him and yourself. If He shows you your marriage or other relationships, don't be easy on yourself. If you have children, look closely at what they have become because of you.

Throw the life jacket off, and swim out in the deep. Seeing yourself would be scary if you were alone. You are not alone. That's the point. You have been alone, and now you are not. The height of God's presence and the depth of His love are at your fingertips. Let perseverance finish its work, until you don't lack anything.

Listen carefully. Hear the voice of the angel say, "Now, go in the strength that you have and deliver, rescue, and encourage. The Lord is with you, mighty warrior." Press into God, and He will come to you.

18

LEAVING A LEGACY

Passing Your Faith to the Next Generation

J. D. KING

A few years ago, I was holding my son in one of the outpouring services in Kansas City. The powerful stirrings of the Lord could be felt throughout the room. Many who had gathered for this service were on their faces, crying out to God. It felt as if electricity was shooting through my bloodstream. Everything was invigorating and alive.

While all of this was transpiring, I asked my young son, "Can you feel the presence of God?"

A sheepish look came on his face, and he said, "No, Daddy . . . I don't feel anything."

I must admit, that wasn't the response I had hoped for. I assumed that my son was having the same kind of encounter that I was in that moment, but he wasn't. After he spoke, I remembered a line I'd heard years before from an elderly believer: "God doesn't have any grandchildren—only sons and daughters."

No one enters the Kingdom of God solely on the coattails of his or her parents. Their family name or illustrious background is not enough to carry people over the threshold. Everyone must become part of the Lord's household directly—as a son or daughter. If this doesn't occur, an individual will miss out on the marvelous things God intends for him or her.

The stirrings of God are supposed to go beyond a single generation. Solomon declared, "Children's children are the crown of old men" (Proverbs 17:6 NKJV). A spiritual inheritance is supposed to be passed down to our children and grandchildren.

Not only should we grow in our awareness and intimacy with the Lord, but so should our bloodline. From the beginning, God intended for us to be image bearers, reflecting His goodness and glory. In real life, we don't see this happening as often as it should. A husband and wife might walk in the glory of the Lord, but their children don't always experience the same reality. There should be a transference, but it is rarer than it should be. Moves of God may shift and change, but they are not supposed to cease. The Kingdom of God is to be forcefully advancing.

The Family Snare

Gideon was blessed and favored by God, but over time he missed part of what he was called to do. He got so caught up in the short term that he messed up part of his legacy. Sloppiness can undermine an otherwise wonderful move of God.

Gideon had the power of the Lord come upon him several times, but he forgot what it meant to be led by the Lord. While he should have been positioning his family—and all Israel—for success, he got off the mark. The spoils of Israel's victories against the Midianites were gathered and turned into a gold ephod, an expensive priestly garment. God never told Gideon to do this, but he got caught up in his own concerns. Scripture declares, "Gideon made the gold into an ephod, which he placed in Ophrah, his town. All

Israel prostituted themselves by worshiping it there, and it became a snare to Gideon and his family" (Judges 8:27 NIV).

Israel turned something designed for good into a worthless idol. These and other wrong moves affected Gideon and his family and also hurt the rest of the nation. Scripture says that the people "prostituted themselves." That outcome is horrific to think about. It's awful when godly people begin to twist and distort the good things God has given them. Many are more in love with the forms than the substance.

Sadly, Gideon didn't make the investments in his family that he should have, and when he died, his sons and all Israel returned to treacherous idol worship. In one generation, his legacy was virtually erased: "As soon as Gideon died, the Israelites prostituted themselves by worshiping the images of Baal, making Baal-berith their god. They forgot the LORD their God, who had rescued them from all their enemies surrounding them" (Judges 8:33–34 NLT).

Gideon had many admirable qualities. His ability to cultivate a deep connection with God and move forward under the Spirit's guidance was commendable. His unwavering courage in the face of political oppression and malevolence inspired an entire nation. Although Gideon did many things right, he ultimately failed in his calling as a father. God's spiritual warrior didn't pass down the wisdom he had gained at the water's edge. Gideon had won virtually all of the short-term battles, but he forgot an equally important matter—the spiritual stature of his sons and daughters. Legacies matter.

Leaving a Legacy Isn't Easy

The challenge of passing a spiritual heritage on to the next generation isn't the only thing Gideon struggled with. There are similar stories throughout the Bible. Scripture makes it clear that leaving a vital spiritual legacy isn't easy.

After the deaths of Joshua and his elders, the nation of Israel had to wrestle with passing the covenant down to the next generations—each family line to the children and grandchildren. Scripture declares, "Israel served the LORD all the days of Joshua, and all the days of the elders who outlived Joshua, who had known all the works of the LORD which He had done for Israel" (Joshua 24:31 NKJV).

As long as those spiritual fathers who knew the presence of the Lord remained at the helm, Israel held onto the ways of God. But for some reason, these men didn't transfer what they knew. When they died, other men rose who didn't know the rhythms or patterns of the Lord. At that time, the nation turned away from all that is holy.

During an earlier era of the judges, we see a similar occurrence. When those who had encountered the Lord's power passed from the earth, their children didn't follow their ways. The Bible affirms, "After that generation died, another generation grew up who did not acknowledge the LORD or remember the mighty things he had done for Israel" (Judges 2:10 NLT).

When those who have known the presence of the Lord pass from the earth, spiritual treasures are often lost. This should not be so.

Losing a Legacy

These spiritual breakdowns have been disastrous in the past, and they continue to plague families in our day. It breaks my heart when I witness kids walking away from a strong spiritual heritage. I've watched it happen over and over.

Several years ago, I had the privilege of observing a devoted father nurturing his daughter. His efforts were tireless. He worked to instill a profound love for God through prayer, encouragement, and daily Scripture readings.

Despite his best intentions, however, his daughter merely went through the motions, never fully embracing Jesus as Lord. While everything appeared good on the surface, cracks began to emerge as the young woman matured and established her own family. Amid the whirlwind of daily life, her interest in spiritual things waned even further, leaving only the remnants of Christianity within her household.

Tragically, this spiritual apathy has extended to this woman's children. They now display an even greater indifference toward God. It's foreseeable that as they come of age, they will likely drift away from the Church and become estranged from their grandfather's legacy. What a horrible thing to witness.

God moves in the hearts of men and women, intending to transform their whole lineage. Yet something can go terribly wrong. Legacies can get lost. This should not be happening in the lives of Spirit-led believers.

When I Hear Broken Prayer

A few years ago, I had the privilege of traveling to the Hebrides islands, off the coast of Scotland. A marvelous move of God broke open from 1949–1953—transforming the lives of hardened shepherds and sailors.

One of the leaders in the revival was a blacksmith named Donald John Smith. He would pray while forging horseshoes and tools. This fervent prayer warrior's tears kept dropping on the hot anvil as he interceded—making a loud sizzling sound. His anointed intercession was quite visceral.

During the revival, Smith had a teenage son who was deeply impacted—becoming just as fervent as his father. When I traveled to the Isle of Lewis in 2009, I met with this now-elderly son. I was shocked to see the holy spark in his eyes. Though aged, he still sought the Lord fervently.

The devout blacksmith had passed his hunger for the Lord down one generation, but it hadn't gone much further. The grandsons and other family seemed to know very little of the glory. While attending worship services at the Barvas Church, the epicenter of the revival decades earlier, the grandchildren of Donald John Smith seemed lethargic and disconnected.

On my last day on the islands, I was able to visit the Smith cottage. Coming in, I walked past the patriarch's weather-beaten anvil by the front gate. When I entered the home, some of the decor and furnishings were the same as they had been in 1949—when the prayer meetings were first hosted there.

The elderly son of the blacksmith served tea and talked about his yearning for a fresh move of God. Trembling, he asserted, "I know that revival will come again to the Hebrides islands!" With tears running down his face, he paused and said, "I know it will come when I hear the sound of broken prayer."

When I heard these words, it cut me to the heart. I wondered if I would recognize the sound of broken prayer. What would I hear if our sons and daughters cried out to the Lord? As I reflected on this, I said to the Lord, *How do I ensure that this moves on to the next generation? Help me light the fire in my children . . .*

Investing in the Future

I want my son to know the goodness and glory of the Lord. I want him to walk in the ways of righteousness. But if I'm going to pass down this legacy, I must make the right kind of spiritual investments. If you and I are going to impart a spiritual thirst to the next generation, we must be willing to do what our ancestors were hesitant to do.

One thing we must do is tell better stories. Throughout Scripture, the righteous were instructed to keep the testimony. The Bible says, "Blessed are those who keep His testimonies, who seek Him with the whole heart!" (Psalm 119:2 NKJV). It's important to recount the marvelous acts you have witnessed. Talk about them over and over. In Deuteronomy, Moses said, "Only be careful, and watch yourselves closely so that you do not forget the things your eyes have seen or let them fade from your heart as long as you live. Teach them to your children and to their children after them" (Deuteronomy 4:9 NIV).

We rightly long for our children to believe in Jesus and to possess a deep, unwavering faith. But to get there, our kids will need more than mere behaviorism and moral precepts. Young people must encounter dynamic, spiritually charged stories. Nothing is transformed in this life by empty words. In the end, our sons and daughters will align with whoever offers the most compelling stories and songs.

We also need spaces that welcome deep encounters with the Lord. Believers should endeavor to cultivate spiritual atmospheres at home and in other spheres—places where genuine connection and breakthroughs can occur.

To secure a lasting spiritual heritage for generations to come, it's crucial to cultivate environments rich in the goodness and glory of the Lord. These spaces should serve as welcoming hubs positioned for our sons and daughters to come face-to-face with Jesus. Believers must nurture within their homes and in other spheres the conditions where deep connections and life changes are possible.

Have you prayed and welcomed the Lord to come into the rooms you walk into? We need to start at home, but we also try to do this in the places where we gather for worship. A poignant example of this occurs in the book of Acts. Believers who loved the Lord prayed and expected the entire room to shift:

"Stretch out your hand to heal and perform signs and wonders through the name of your holy servant Jesus."

After they prayed, the place where they were meeting was shaken. And they were all filled with the Holy Spirit and spoke the word of God boldly.

Acts 4:30–31 NIV

These believers weren't meeting in a synagogue or a church building; they were gathered in a home. I'm thankful when glory falls in a church, but we need the Lord in every realm of our lives. Don't overlook the importance of cultivating the smaller rooms.

Can you help foster spaces and moments that will invite your family into the goodness and love of the Father? The Lord wants to get parents and kids walking side by side.

Allowing Breathing Room

Amid all of this, we must remember that when our kids experience God, it probably won't look the same as our encounters. There may be different manifestations and phenomena. We might not always feel comfortable with what's occurring. Yet real mothers and fathers know they must loosen their grip if they want their children to have life-changing encounters. Those who are emerging will always experience different things than those who went before them. It's important to allow space for the Holy Spirit to move as He sees fit.

Amazing encounters can occur when parents and overseers allow breathing room. Godly mothers and fathers must allow space for their kids' unique expressions and experiences. Many believers who are mature in their faith seem to confuse their personal preferences with divine mandates. Those more established in the things of God often assume that their tone and worship expressions will be emulated. These shortsighted expectations fail to account for the unique journeys and perspectives of their family.

Passing a spiritual legacy on to your children and grandchildren isn't about a particular methodology or style. The Lord isn't overly concerned about the fashions people wear or the style of music they play. Sadly, such are the myriads of things Christians waste their time arguing about. The individuals who are in charge must let go of their own interests and work to champion the needs of the emerging generations.

I often see situations where older believers need to rethink their responses. For example, those who grew up in intact families don't understand the pains of a fatherless generation. Many young people are grappling with identity issues. If we want the next generation to experience Jesus, we shouldn't dismiss all their felt needs. Be careful that you don't reject what God is doing in this hour because it offends your sensibilities. A move of God often emerges along the edge of cultural fault lines.

Whether you like it or not, movements move. If you aren't advancing with the purposes of God in this hour, you're probably falling behind. When the prophet Jeremiah witnessed people "following the stubborn desires of their evil hearts," he asserted, under the leading of the Holy Spirit, that they were going "backward instead of forward" (Jeremiah 7:24 NLT). I imagine a Spirit-led prophet would make a similar assertion about some today.

What God is up to in this hour, in the nations, transcends all our personal preferences. An outpouring of the Holy Spirit that impacts our kids is probably never going to fit into the neat little boxes we've set aside for it. Disruptions are inevitable. Centuries ago, Jesus made it clear that He has no problem overturning tables in the house of God (see Matthew 21:12). So don't let anything man-made stand in the way of the glory.

It's crucial to recognize that some of the disruptions that unsettle the mature might captivate the younger generations. The Lord's surprising works can seize the hearts of the masses. In the era of the prophet Haggai, God promised to "shake all the nations" and in doing so, "fill this place with glory" (Haggai 2:7 NLT). We don't always like it, but the glory often comes after the shaking.

If we desire a better future for our children, we must lean into the Lord's mysterious angles and trajectories. You should already know by now that the legacy being forged on earth isn't centered around us. In Ezekiel's time, God emphasized that His marvelous acts weren't about validating those already in the know. It was about having the unbelieving masses turn their gaze to the Lord.

The Lord declared through the prophet, "It is not for your sake, people of Israel, that I am going to do these things, but for the sake of my holy name" (Ezekiel 36:22 NIV).

Spiritual power and truth are not for wielding political power or condemning outsiders. Grace emerges so that God's Kingdom can permeate every corner of our world. Everyone, both inside and outside the fold, should be witnessing the goodness and mercy of the Lord. Let me assure you that your kids know when it's more about you than it is about God.

Passing Down an Inheritance

When I held my son a few years ago and imagined what things might be like in the future, I made a firm commitment: *I will do all I can to cultivate an atmosphere of glory.* I'm sure there are going to be things in the future that I'll struggle with. I'm not always going to be comfortable with where things are going. The moves of God on the horizon will probably disrupt my sensibilities. What will transpire in my automobile or home might not be like anything I've experienced before. I might even find myself feeling uncomfortable. Nevertheless, I trust in the heavenly Father and His unimaginable goodness. I know He will do amazing things with my son and those from his generation.

I'd like for my son to encounter God through me. On some level, I know he has. Yet there are limits to how far my experiences can take him. He's standing in an entirely different place than I am. It's difficult to pass a spiritual inheritance down to the next generation, but I'm determined to give it everything I have.

Over the last few years, I've read the Scriptures with my son and have recounted some of the marvelous things that I've witnessed. I invite him to dialogue with me and ask plenty of questions. I've tried to do this with my daughter as well. My children know that I pray for them every day. I don't always do everything right, and I've made plenty of mistakes, but I know that God's goodness and grace can make up for my deficiencies. I believe that my children will carry the name of Jesus to the next generation.

From Glory to Glory

Throughout history, Gideon and many others failed to recognize the significance of leaving a legacy. It's challenging to find examples of mothers and fathers who have transmitted their commitment to a spiritual fervor effectively to the next generation. Although individuals may personally experience the transformative power of God's glory, they often struggle to convey this reality to their own children.

I believe that God will assist us in overcoming these obstacles and will grant us the wisdom to succeed where others have fallen short. I have faith that we will not only taste the beginnings of a glorious move of God, but will also witness its continuation in the lives of our children and grandchildren. The Holy Spirit will empower us to leave glorious legacies.

It's time to impart the goodness and awe-inspiring nature of the Lord to the next generation. Will you lay a spiritual foundation that will not crumble for those who are not yet born?

19

RIPPLES IN THE WATER

Passing the River Test

▌ J. D. KING

As Gideon and his men congregated at the river's edge, they found themselves wrestling not only with their thirst, but also with the weight of destiny. Shorelines aren't just resting places; they are also where people are consecrated, activated, and released.

With each sip drawn from the stream, a metamorphosis transpires, shaping parched souls into mighty warriors. In the depths of darkness, the resilient rise, propelled by the leadings of the Holy Spirit. These are the ones who listen, pray, and move in the Spirit's anointing.

The biblical narratives have so many layers that help us see who we are and what we need to do. Within the rich tapestry of Scripture, Gideon's story is a prophetic parable, helping us grapple with our own identity and longings. Through his saga, we glean wisdom and inspiration.

Wheat threshers like Gideon show us that moving forward in victory necessitates adequate times of preparation. The waters aren't merely about comfort; they symbolize the sifting and re-ordering of one's life. Before you or I can access, we will need to learn how to process. The Lord is positioning us to learn and grow so we can receive everything He has for us.

The story of Gideon shows us that thirsty souls ought to adopt a posture of receptivity—understanding that the journey demands more than just casual sipping. Those who desire more in the Kingdom of God must learn to drink deeply. It's an arduous journey, but essential to nurture what the Spirit is activating within.

An Inexplicable Glory

I stand humbled by the force of the river. It serves as a catalyst for remarkable transformations. The invigorating streams wash over believers, making the intangible tangible. With each ebb and flow, the river carries away the remnants of yesteryears, ushering in new life.

Amid the waters, I've been privileged to witness awe-inspiring moments. Once we are touched by God, the mundane loses its appeal. Why would I ever want to go back to the way things were before? The river changes everything.

Steve Gray and I often find ourselves reflecting on the moments when God has drawn near. Many have asked us about our experiences and urged us to discuss what we've seen. Indeed, the stories of our encounters could probably fill several volumes. The river of revival touches individuals in so many ways.

For example, I knew a factory worker who received a fiery touch from God. He began regularly to cry out in intercession, asking Jesus to move. At one point, the presence of the Lord so enveloped him in his home that he couldn't stand. He collapsed under the weightiness of God in his dining room, knocking over chairs and place settings. While he was on the floor, he pleaded with God to burn out all the sin and dross. Later that evening, when he got into bed, he began trembling. This continued after he fell asleep. When his wife touched him to make sure he was okay, she began shaking as well. For a week, they could barely speak because the Lord was moving so mightily on them. Let me tell you, the glory of the Lord was evident in that household.

I've also witnessed moments when children were overcome by the glory of the Lord. On several occasions, my own kids got wide-eyed, claiming to witness angels and other spiritual realities. They described beautiful colors and lights racing through the room. Their compelling and credible accounts aren't the only ones I've heard. Many young people have entered the deeper places with God.

I knew a three-year-old who could quote Scripture and move prophetically. Many times, he accurately discerned the heart of the Lord. Once, he got upset when some adults resisted the work of the Spirit. He pleaded with them to honor the Lord, and when they responded to his urgings, God began to change the atmosphere.

This boy's sister, who was just a few years older, felt led to pray for the sick. On one occasion, a knee was healed when the young girl laid her hands on the ailment. Scripture reminds us that God has hidden the things of the Kingdom "from the wise and learned, and revealed them to little children" (Matthew 11:25 NIV).

I have also witnessed incredibly profound moments when people have gathered in worship. In an electrifying atmosphere, individuals might respond in various ways. For example, I have heard loud shrieks, witnessed speaking in tongues, and observed people weeping uncontrollably—often accompanied by intense trembling. Some individuals even entered a trance-like state, remaining motionless as they communed with God. The river can truly be overwhelming.

I recall one occasion when I caught a glimpse of the glory cloud in the upper reaches of a sanctuary. The crowd felt the weightiness, and many fell on their faces. In a similar encounter, what the ancient Jews called the *kavod* overpowered Moses. Scripture says that he "could not enter the tent of meeting because the cloud had settled on it" (Exodus 40:35 NIV). When I saw this happen, one man was so awestruck by it that he fled the building and locked himself in his car.

During a time when the glory cloud was evident, young children witnessed angels moving through the room. One young girl sensed that these spiritual beings were part of a heavenly entourage fighting for the souls of the people. The more the congregation prayed, the faster the angels seemed to move. In Scripture, God is referred to as Lord of the angelic hosts (see Joshua 5:14–15; Psalm 103:21). So wherever He appears, the heavenly entourage typically travels alongside Him.

Steve Gray sometimes would draw attention to the open heavens during services, and when this happened, people would witness indescribable things. On one occasion, a pastor had an open vision. He saw what looked like a stairway from heaven. Hundreds, if not thousands, of angels raced down into the throng of earthly worshipers. This pastor wrote,

> I saw hundreds, perhaps even thousands, of angels . . . coming down the stairs; right into the midst of the worship service. . . . It seemed that the angels were rushing, scrambling, and attempting to climb over each another . . . in a hurry to make it into the worship service. From there, the angels gathered around the congregation, about ten to twelve feet off the ground. They remained and worshipped with us the entire time. It was truly joy unspeakable and full of glory.[1]

Whether someone is encountering the glory of the Lord in the solitude of his or her bedroom or amid the worship of a church, it is invigorating. In a move of God, living waters can flow through every crevice, penetrating into the fabric of people's lives. These overwhelming experiences change everything.

Not the Falling, But the Getting Up

Gideon and countless others have been drawn in by the mesmerizing allure of the river. Many have found it difficult to avert their gaze. Recently, a friend approached me with a series of questions about these waters. He wondered whether I thought that a move of God was primarily about sensational encounters. He wanted to know what I meant by the river.

I acknowledged that when the Spirit of God stirs, people get overwhelmed. Many are shaken whenever the Lord steps down from heaven. The inexplicable glory of God will always capture the attention of the masses. It's difficult to look away when the Holy Spirit shows up. Yet, there is something else at stake when we come to the river.

Underneath the spectacle, a genuine outpouring of the Holy Spirit centers on Jesus' enduring impact. Although I've seen many marvelous displays over the years, what still resonates are the transformations. Fundamentally, the river of revival is about a radical life change. It's not the falling, but the changes that occur when people get back up.

I've witnessed individuals undergoing changes that have left a lasting mark on their lives. For example, there was a single mom who had everything going wrong in her life. Yet in the glorious river, all things became new. She gave up a life of sin and discovered her destiny as an intercessor. Whenever she prayed for people, the chains fell off and their minds were freed. She was so dynamic in her intercession that many wanted her to minister to them. This woman became a catalyst for thousands finding freedom. She is still making a difference in so many lives.

I remember when a deeply tormented person sought solace in the living waters. Over several years, this individual grappled with multiple "personalities" that sporadically surfaced. A group of intercessors raised their voices in prayer, and as they pressed in, most of the dark spirits vacated. Yet one held on. It defiantly proclaimed, "I don't have to leave. I'm the big one."

227

Kathy Gray, the wife of Steve Gray, was spearheading the prayer effort. She asserted, "God is bigger! Go, in the name of Jesus!"

Immediately, the victimized person regained lost innocence, and remains free to this day.

The stories are endless. A former drug addict, suffering from brain fog, experienced restoration in the presence of the Holy Spirit. Jesus touched his life, and he committed himself to the Lord. This man, who could barely communicate, completed college and built a million-dollar business. God recognized the incredible potential within him and continues to position him for earthshaking things today. The Lord is a restorer.

Among my favorite accounts is that of a woman who returned from combat overseas. Although she had been raised in the Church, she had drifted away from the Lord and embraced an alternative lifestyle. Although things were going the wrong way, Jesus intervened. Her trauma and pain were washed away in the mercies of the Lord. All at once, she received a fresh start. It's truly awe-inspiring to witness how the love of God can transform every aspect of a person's life.

The stories continue to pour in—a constant stream of individuals finding wholeness by the river's edge. I'm rarely surprised by the testimonies, but every now and then, one makes me pause. Not too long ago, Jim, one of the seminarians who made the trek to Smithton in the late 1990s, reached out on social media. He said he has never forgotten what he witnessed during his visit. The living waters stay with people long after the streams run dry.

Passing the River Test

Centuries ago, a band of weary warriors drank from a life-giving stream. As they quenched their parched throats, they altered the course of Israel's history. In a singular moment, the mundane transcended into the miraculous. Ordinary individuals were roused to victory.

Gideon's saga whispers across the chasm of time, carrying with it lessons that continue to resonate. He shows us that the living waters do not merely cleanse and refresh; they also reshape the identity and trajectory of a whole new generation. In these waters, men and women still come alive.

Now, as you stand on the banks of the river, you are faced with a choice. It's a challenge that echoes through the ages. Will you, like Gideon's valiant few, drink deeply from the living waters? Will you grab hold of that which beckons you?

Individuals who pass the river test have not only determined their thirst, but they have also determined their destiny.

ACKNOWLEDGMENTS

Creating a book is a journey that thrives on collaboration, and this book is no exception. Our deepest gratitude goes to Kathy Gray, whose insights and dedication have profoundly shaped this manuscript.

We also extend a special thank-you to David Sluka, whose efforts were crucial in bringing our vision to life on these pages.

To the vibrant community at Revive Church in Kansas City, your steadfast support and encouragement have been our guiding light. Your blessings have truly made this endeavor possible, and we are forever thankful.

NOTES

Chapter 1 Summoned to the River

1. Email sent to Smithton Community Church, July 17, 1998.

2. See the following: Joel Kilpatrick, "Revival Rocks Small Missouri Town: People are Traveling Thousands of Miles to Visit a Church in the Town of Smithton, Population 532," *Charisma*, May 1997, 22–23. Joel Kilpatrick, "Revival in the Middle of Nowhere," *Charisma*, February 1998, 46–51. John W. Kennedy, "The Cornfield Revival: For Two Years, Thousands Have Been Leaping For Joy," *Christianity Today*, April 6, 1998. Kenneth L. Woodward, with Peter Annin and Beth Dickey, "Living in the Holy Spirit," *Newsweek*, April 13, 1998, 54–60. Edward M. Eveld, "Moved by the Spirit: Thousands Drawn to 'Revival in the Middle of Nowhere,'" *Kansas City Star*, FYI Section, July 24, 1998, 1, 14. Don Lattin, "Revival Fever Rising," *San Francisco Chronicle*, September 18, 1999, 1, 15.

3. Samuel Autman, "Revival in the Land," *St. Louis Post-Dispatch*, June 7, 1998.

Chapter 3 Fervent Cries

1. Samuel Chadwick, *25 Sunday Mornings with Samuel Chadwick* (London: The Epworth Press, 1952), 102.

2. A. T. Pierson and J. Edwin Orr, quoted in Austen C. Ukachi, "Revival is a product of intense prayer," *The Guardian*, May 12, 2019, https://guardian.ng/sunday-magazine/revival-is-a-product-of-intense-prayer/.

3. Kenneth S. Wuest, *The New Testament: An Expanded Translation* (Grand Rapids: William B. Eerdmans Publishing Company, 1961), 353.

4. This was translator Emily Chisholm's summary of Tersteegen's teachings, found in her "Translator's Preface" in Gerhard Tersteegen, *The Quiet Way: A Christian Path to Inner Peace*, trans. Emily Chisholm (Bloomington, Indiana: World Wisdom, 2008), ix–x.

5. Corey Russell, *Foundations of Intercession, Course Notes* (Kansas City: Forerunner Publishing, 2013), 6.

6. A. W. Tozer, *Keys to the Deeper Life,* rev. and expanded (Grand Rapids: Zondervan Publishing House, 1988), 22–23.

7. Samuel Chadwick, *The Path of Prayer* (Kansas City: Beacon Hill, 1931), 65.

Chapter 4 In the Winepress

1. Billy Graham, "Answers," *Kansas City Star,* November 27, 2006; see also https://billygraham.org/answer/do-you-think-theres-any-hope-of-reversing-all -these-problems-with-our-political-system/.

Chapter 6 Rattling Bones and Small Clouds

1. Madison Pierce's Facebook page, February 15, 2023, https://www.facebook .com/madison.pierce.353/posts/5872048629538971?ref=embed_post.

2. Ibid.

3. Ibid.

4. Ibid.

5. Ibid.

6. Lester Sumrall, *Pioneers of Faith* (South Bend, Ind.: LeSea Publishing, 1995), 16.

7. John Wimber, *Everyone Gets to Play: John Wimber's Teaching and Writings on Life Together in Christ* (Boise, Idaho: Ampelon, 2008), 42–43.

8. Arthur Wallis, *In the Day of Thy Power: The Scriptural Principles of Revival* (London: Christian Literature Crusade, 1956, 1961), 10.

Chapter 8 Fleeces and Supernatural Leadings

1. Charles G. Finney, "What a Revival of Religion Is," in *Lectures on Revivals of Religion,* 6th ed. (New York: Leavitt, Lord & Co., 1835), 12.

Chapter 9 A Sound from Heaven

1. Frank Bartleman, *How Pentecost Came to Los Angeles: As It Was In the Beginning* (Los Angeles: Bartleman, 1925), 58.

2. A. W. Otto, describing a Maria Woodworth-Etter meeting, referenced in Richard Riss, "The Heavenly Choir," *The International Pentecostal Holiness Church Advocate,* Summer 1996, no. 2, 2, https://pentecostalarchives.org /?a=d&d=IPHCA199607-01.1.1&e=.

3. See Malcolm Miller, "The Shofar and its Symbolism," *Historic Brass Society Journal* 14 (2002): 88. See also https://www.historicbrass.org/edocman/hbj-2002 /HBSJ_2002_JL01_005_Miller.pdf.

4. Michael Strassfeld, "Traditions for Rosh Ha-Shanah," in *The Jewish Holy Days* (New York: Harper & Row, 1985), 99.

5. James Finley, as quoted in Michael McClymond, "Embodying the Spirit: New Perspectives on North American Revivalism," *Journal of American History* 92:3 (December 2005): 984.

6. S. B. Shaw, *The Great Revival in Wales* (Chicago: Shaw, 1905), 11.

Chapter 10 Refreshing Streams

1. John Wesley quoted in E.M. Bounds, *The Possibilities of Prayer* (Grand Rapids: Baker, 1979), 138.

2. Jonathan Edwards, "The Distinguishing Marks of a Work of the Spirit of God," *Jonathan Edwards on Revival* (Edinburgh: The Banner of Truth Trust, 1987), 37.

3. Charles Grandison Finney, *The Original Memoirs of Charles G. Finney*, eds. Garth M. Rosell and Richard A. G. Dupuis (Grand Rapids: Zondervan, 1989, 2002), 16.

4. Ibid., 82–83.

5. Vinson Synan, as quoted in Richard N. Ostling, "Laughing for the Lord: Revivalist fervor has invaded the Church of England," *Time*, August 15, 1994, 38, https://time.com/vault/issue/1994-08-15/page/40/.

6. John Long, "Joy (Burst On Out)," Revive Music, 2020. See also Revive Music, John Long, "Joy (Burst On Out) [Acoustic]," 3:36, posted by ReviveMusicVEVO, May 6, 2022, https://www.youtube.com/watch?v=bd3J3b7is0M.

Chapter 13 The Now Moment

1. John Wesley, journal entry referenced in C. A. Waterfield, "Lost: John Wesley," *The Methodist Review* 62 (1913): 750.

2. Frank Bartleman, *How Pentecost Came to Los Angeles: As it Was in the Beginning,* 2nd ed. (Los Angeles: Frank Bartleman, 1925), 65. See also https://ccel.org/ccel/bartleman/los/Page_65.html.

Chapter 16 God Disruptions

1. Dwain Carter, "Slain in Smithton," *Word&Way*, March 25, 1999, 7.

2. Arthur Wallis, *In the Day of Thy Power* (Fort Washington, Penn.: CLC Publications, 1956, 2010), 31.

3. William Alexander McKay, *Outpourings of the Spirit: Or, A Narrative of Spiritual Awakenings in Different Ages and Countries* (Philadelphia: Presbyterian Board of Publication, 1890), 21.

4. Charles F. Parham, "Sermon by Chas. F. Parham. Portland, Ore. Nov. 15, 1924," *Apostolic Faith* 1, no. 3 (April 1925): 9, https://digitalshowcase.oru.edu/apostolic_faith/6/.

5. John Johnson, quoted in Susannah Johnson, *Recollections of the Rev. John Johnson and His Home* (Nashville: Southern Methodist Publishing House, 1869), 27.

6. Unnamed circuit rider, quoted in Henry Smith, *Recollections and Reflections of an Old Itinerant: A Series of Letters* (New York: Carlton & Phillips, 1854), 31–32.

7. James A. Stewart, *Invasion of Wales by the Spirit Through Evan Roberts* (Asheville, N.C.: Revival Literature, 1963, 2004), 29.

8. Duncan Campbell, *The Lewis Awakening, 1949–1953* (Edinberg, Scotland: The Faith Mission, 1954), 29–30.

9. D. Martyn Lloyd-Jones, quoted in John White, *When the Spirit Comes with Power: Signs & Wonders among God's People* (Downers Grove, Ill.: InterVarsity Press, 1988), 13.

10. John Wimber with Keven Springer, *Power Evangelism* (San Francisco: Harper & Row, 1986), 71.

11. John Wesley, journal entry dated July 7, 1739, in *The Journal of the Rev. John Wesley*, vol. 1, (London: J. M. Dent & Sons, 1906, 1913, 1921, 1930), 210. See also HathiTrust, "The Journal of the Rev. John Wesley v.1," https://babel .hathitrust.org/cgi/pt?id=mdp.39015041157986&seq=230.

12. John Wesley, journal entry dated November 25, 1759, in, *The Journal of The Rev. John Wesley, A.M. in Four Vols.*, Vol. II (London: Dent & Co., 1906), 489.

Chapter 19 Ripples in the Water

1. Email to Smithton Community Church, December 11, 1998.

STEVE GRAY is a multifaceted individual with a diverse range of accomplishments. A seasoned pastor and sought-after speaker, his spiritual guidance and leadership have touched multiple thousands. As founding lead pastor of Revive Church in Kansas City, Missouri, he oversees a large team and vibrant congregation. He made his mark leading the Smithton Outpouring of 1996 and the Kansas City Revival of 2008.

As a writer, Steve has authored works which resonate with readers seeking understanding of revival, awakening, and the Kingdom of God. In filmmaking and television, he is a three-time Emmy award winner, showcasing his ability to create compelling content. Steve's creativity also extends to music. With multiple releases as a songwriter and recording artist, he has enriched many through his music.

Steve's dedication to education is demonstrated by his lifetime teaching certificate in Missouri and his doctorate in theology. He holds a bachelor's degree in instrumental/vocal music and education. Additionally, Steve founded Lee's Summit Academy, as well as Libby Lane Preschool & Montessori.

Steve's dedication to his family shines through his fifty-year marriage to his wife, Kathy, as well as his pride in being a parent to two daughters and a grandfather to five cherished grandchildren.

CONNECT WITH STEVE:

SteveGrayMinistries.com   Steve Gray Ministries   @PastorSteveGray

Steve Gray   @_StevenJGray_

More Faith More Life Podcast:

@mfml.pod

J. D. KING is a seasoned leader who has functioned in diverse roles over the decades. Presently, he is a pastor at Revive Church in Kansas City.

Before assuming his present positions, J. D. was the international director of the Revival Network of Ministries and the academic dean for the Revival Training Center. Having traveled across North America as an itinerant minister, he has had the opportunity to engage with many congregations.

J. D.'s passion for leadership and spiritual empowerment extends to the written word. Some of his articles have been featured in *Charisma*, *Spirit-Led Woman*, and *Pneuma Review*. In addition, J. D.'s blog posts have been widely shared, accumulating over 1.5 million page views. J. D. has written six books and contributed to four others. In 2017, he founded Christos Publishing, a company dedicated to producing superbly researched books informed by a Spirit-led worldview.

J. D. and his wife, Bobbie, have been married for nearly thirty years, and they reside in Lee's Summit, Missouri, with their kids.

CONNECT WITH J. D.:

 JDKing.net J.D. King

 @jdking @jdkinginsights